Collins

INTERNATIONAL
PRIMARY
SCIENCE

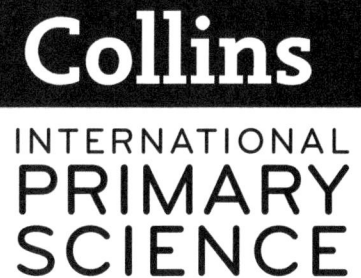

Teacher's Guide 3

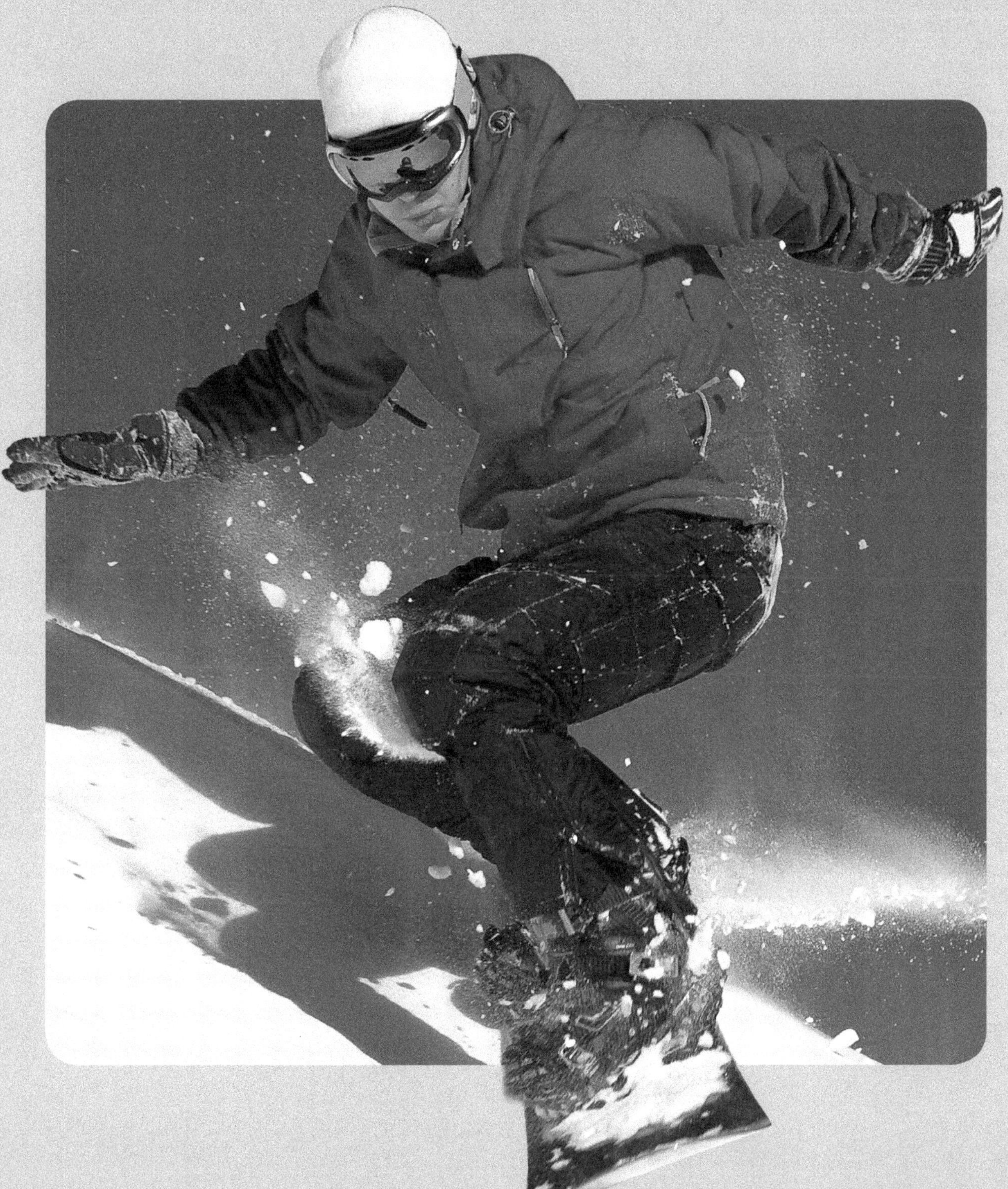

William Collins' dream of knowledge for all began with the publication of his first book in 1819. A self-educated mill worker, he not only enriched millions of lives, but also founded a flourishing publishing house. Today, staying true to this spirit, Collins books are packed with inspiration, innovation and practical expertise. They place you at the centre of a world of possibility and give you exactly what you need to explore it.

Collins. Freedom to teach.

Published by Collins
An imprint of HarperCollins*Publishers* Ltd.
The News Building
1 London Bridge Street
London
SE1 9GF

Browse the complete Collins catalogue at www.collins.co.uk

© HarperCollins*Publishers* Limited 2014

10 9 8

ISBN: 978-0-00-758617-2

The authors assert their moral rights to be identified as the authors of this work.

Contributing authors: Fiona MacGregor, Karen Morrison, Tracey Baxter, Sunetra Berry, Pat Dower, Helen Harden, Pauline Hannigan, Anita Loughrey, Emily Miller, Jonathan Miller, Anne Pilling, Pete Robinson.

The exam-style questions and sample answers used in the Assessment Sheets have been written by the author.

Any educational institution that has purchased one copy of this publication may make unlimited duplicate copies for use exclusively within that institution. Permission does not extend to reproduction, storage within a retrieval system, or transmittal in any form or by any means, electronic, mechanical, photocopying, recording or otherwise, of duplicate copies for loaning, renting or selling to any other institution without the permission of the Publisher.

British Library Cataloguing in Publication Data
A Catalogue record for this publication is available from the British Library.

Commissioned by Elizabeth Catford
Project managed by Karen Williams
Design and production by Ken Vail Graphic Design

Acknowledgements
The publishers wish to thank the following for permission to reproduce photographs.
Every effort has been made to trace copyright holders and to obtain their permission for the use of copyright materials. The publishers will gladly receive any information enabling them to rectify any error or omission at the firsto pportunity.

COVER: Logutenko / Shutterstock.com

All other photos Shutterstock.

Contents

Introduction	v
Teacher's Guide	vi
Student's Book	viii
Workbook	x
DVD	xi
Assessment in primary science	xii
Learning objectives matching grid	xiv
Scientific enquiry skills matching grid	xvi

Lesson plans

Topic 1 Plants

1.1	Parts of plants	2
1.2	Plant roots and stems	4
1.3	Plants need water	6
1.4	Plants need sunlight	8
1.5	Plants need warmth	10
1.6	Healthy plants	12
1.7	Water plants	14
1.8	Plants in the desert	16
1.9	Mountain plants	18
1.10	Flowers and unusual plants	20
	Consolidation and Assessment Sheet answers	22
	Student's Book answers	23

Topic 2 Humans and animals

2.1	Life processes	24
2.2	Living and non-living things	26
2.3	Food for energy	28
2.4	Eating the right food	30
2.5	Eating the wrong food	32
2.6	Exercise	34
2.7	Your senses	36
2.8	How your senses help you	38
2.9	Classifying living things (1)	40
2.10	Classifying living things (2)	42
	Consolidation and Assessment Sheet answers	44
	Student's Book answers	45

Topic 3 Material properties

3.1	Properties of materials	46
3.2	Hard or soft?	48
3.3	Strength	50
3.4	Flexibility	52
3.5	Structures	54
3.6	Uses of materials	56
3.7	Staying the same shape	58
3.8	Floating or sinking?	60
3.9	See-through or not?	62
3.10	Wet or dry?	64
3.11	Magnets	66
3.12	Using magnets	68
	Consolidation and Assessment Sheet answers	70
	Student's Book answers	71

Topic 4 Forces and motion

4.1	Pushes and pulls	72
4.2	Making things move	74
4.3	Natural forces	76
4.4	Measuring forces	78
4.5	Stopping and starting	80
4.6	Changing direction	82
4.7	Changing shape	84
4.8	Friction	86
	Consolidation and Assessment Sheet answers	88
	Student's Book answers	89

Photocopy Masters 91

Assessment Sheets 109

Introduction

About *Collins International Primary Science*

Collins International Primary Science is specifically written to fully meet the requirements of the Cambridge Primary Science curriculum framework from Cambridge Assessment International Education and the material has been carefully developed to meet the needs of primary science students and teachers in a range of international contexts.

Content is organised according to the three main strands: Biology, Chemistry and Physics and the skills detailed under the Scientific Enquiry strand are introduced and taught in the context of those areas.

All course materials make use of the fully-integrated digital resources available on the DVD. For example, video clips and slideshows allow students the opportunity to view at first-hand examples of habitats, plants and animals they may not be familiar with from their own country. The interactive activities provide a valuable teaching resource that will engage the students and consolidate learning.

Components of the course

For each of Stages 1 to 6 as detailed in the Cambridge Primary Science Framework, we offer:

- A full colour, highly illustrated and photograph rich Student's Book
- A write-in Workbook linked to the Student's Book
- This comprehensive Teacher's Guide with clear suggestions for using the materials, including the electronic components of the course
- A DVD which contains slideshows, video clips, additional photographs and interactive activities for use in the classroom.

Approach

The course is designed with student-centred learning at its heart. The students conduct investigations with guidance and support from their teacher. Their investigations respond to questions asked by the teacher or asked by the students themselves. They are practical and activity-based, and include observing, questioning, making and testing predictions, collecting and recording simple data, observing patterns and suggesting explanations. Plenty of opportunity is provided for the students to consolidate and apply what they have learned and to relate what they are doing in science to other curriculum areas and the environment in which they live.

Much of the students' work is conducted as paired work or in small groups, in line with international best practice. Activities are designed to be engaging for students and to support teachers in their assessment of student progress and achievement. Each lesson is planned to support clear learning objectives and outcomes, to provide students and teachers with a good view of the learning. The activities within each unit provide opportunities for oral and written feedback by the teacher, peer teaching and peer assessment within small groups.

Throughout the course, there is wide variety of learning experiences on offer. The materials are structured so that they do not impose a rigid structure but rather provide a range of options linked to the learning objectives. Teachers are able to select from these to provide an interesting, exciting and appropriate learning experience that is suited to their particular classroom situations.

Differentiation

Differentiation is clearly built into the lesson plans in this Teacher's Guide and levels are indicated against the Student's Book activities. You will see that the practical activities offer three levels of differentiated demand. The square activities are appropriate for the level of nearly all of the students. The circle questions are appropriate for the level of most of the students (this is the level students should be achieving for this stage). The triangle questions are appropriate for some students of higher ability. Teachers may find that achievement levels vary for different content strands and interest levels. So students who are working at the circle level in Biology may find Chemistry or Physics topics more interesting and/or easier, so they may work at a different level for some of the time.

Teacher's Guide

Each double-page spread covers one unit in the Student's Book. Each unit has a clear structure identified by the *Introduction–Teaching and learning activities–Consolidate and review* sequence.

Scientific enquiry skills from Cambridge Primary curriculum covered in the unit are provided as a useful reference for the teacher.

The main **learning objectives** for this unit.

Resources the teacher will require for this unit.

Classroom equipment the teacher will require for this unit.

Key words are repeated from the Student's Book page for the teacher to reinforce during the unit.

Scientific background – a brief summary of the science background that the teacher may find useful for this unit.

Safety notes and any other useful notes for the teacher appear here.

Introduction – this is the introductory part of the unit where ideas are beginning to be explored and students reflect on prior learning and share objectives.

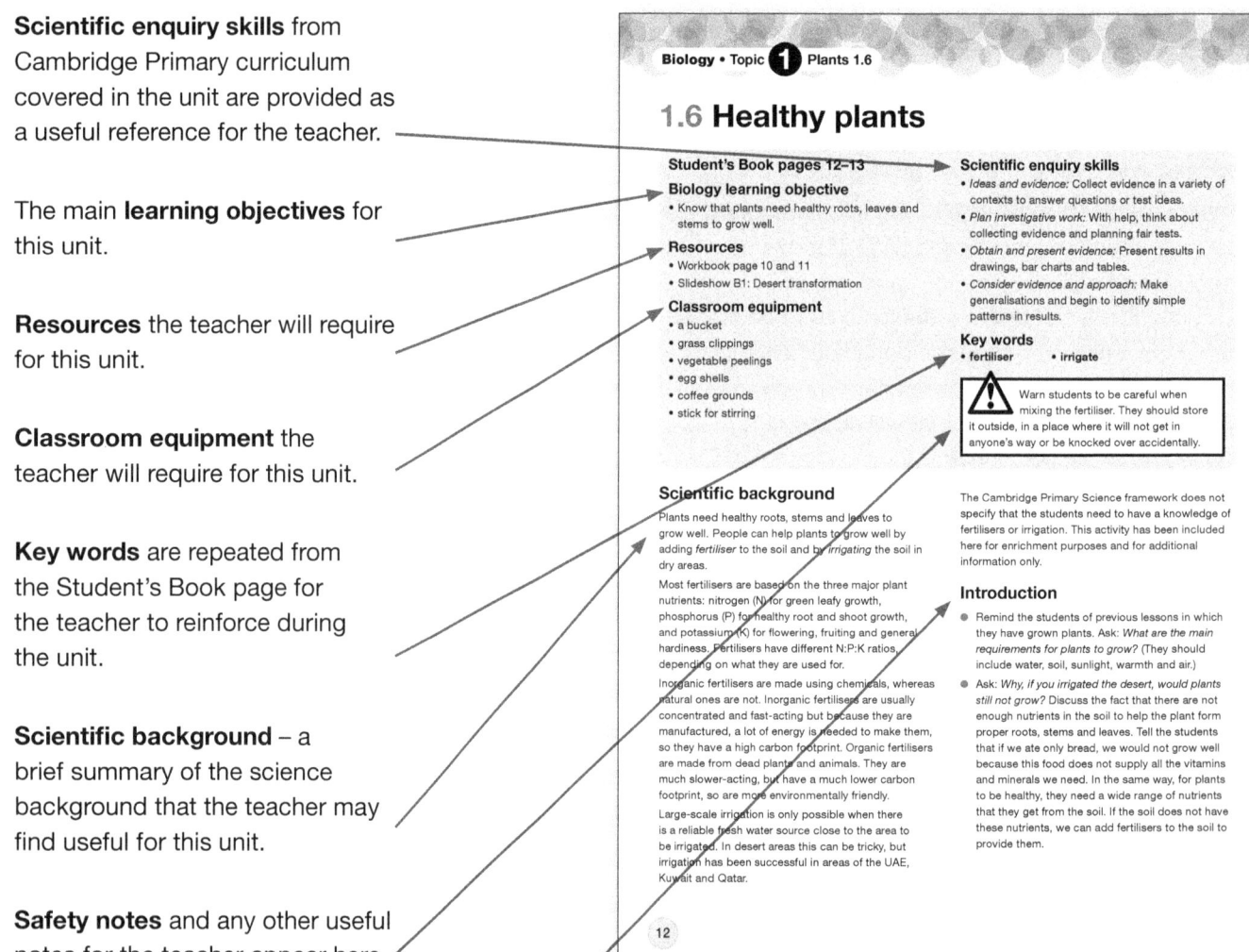

Teacher's Guide

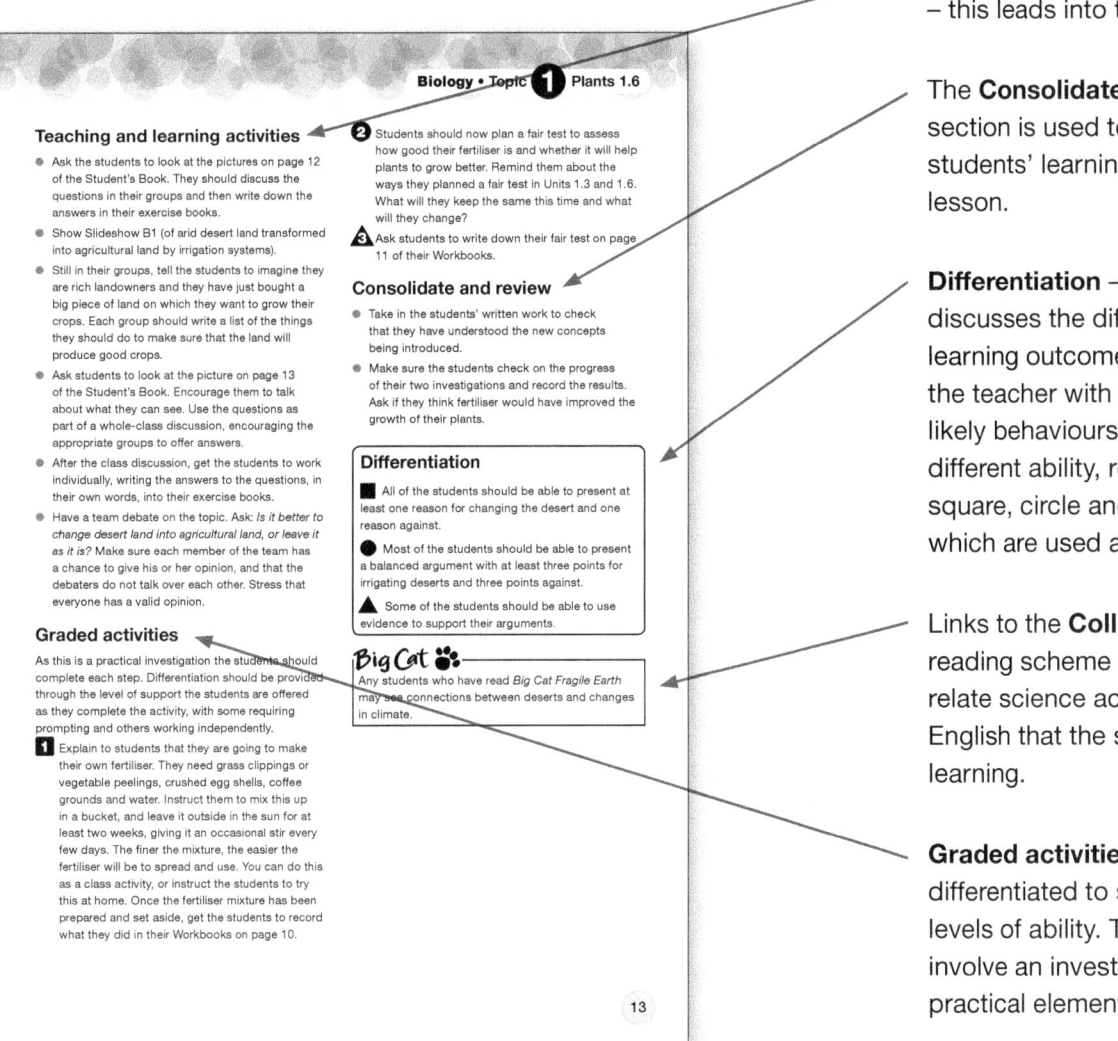

Teaching and learning activities – this leads into the main lesson.

The **Consolidate and review** section is used to reinforce the students' learning during the lesson.

Differentiation – this section discusses the differentiated learning outcomes and provides the teacher with an idea of the likely behaviours of students of different ability, referencing the square, circle and triangle icons which are used across the course.

Links to the **Collins Big Cat** reading scheme are provided to relate science activities to the English that the students are learning.

Graded activities – these are differentiated to suit three different levels of ability. They will often involve an investigation and practical element.

At the end of each Topic the answers to the Student's Book questions and Assessment Sheets are given in full.

At the back of this Teacher's Guide are the Photocopy Masters (PCMs) and Assessment Sheets. These can be photocopied and handed out to the students as necessary.

The Student's Book

Each double page spread covers one unit. Each page has photographs or graphics to provide a stimulus for discussions and questions.

Key words – these are the words that the students will learn and use for this unit.

Questions – These can be used as whole class discussion points and also to enable the teacher to assess how well individual students understand the unit.

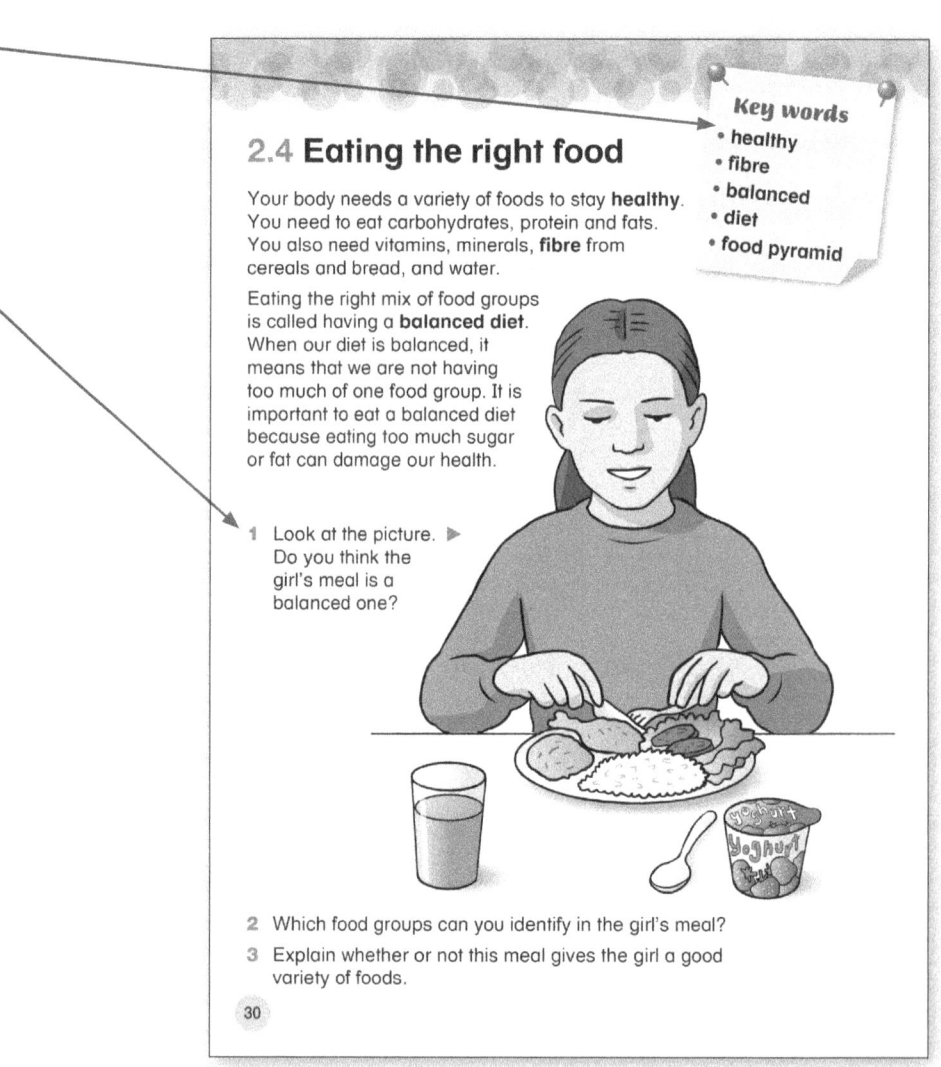

viii

Student's Book

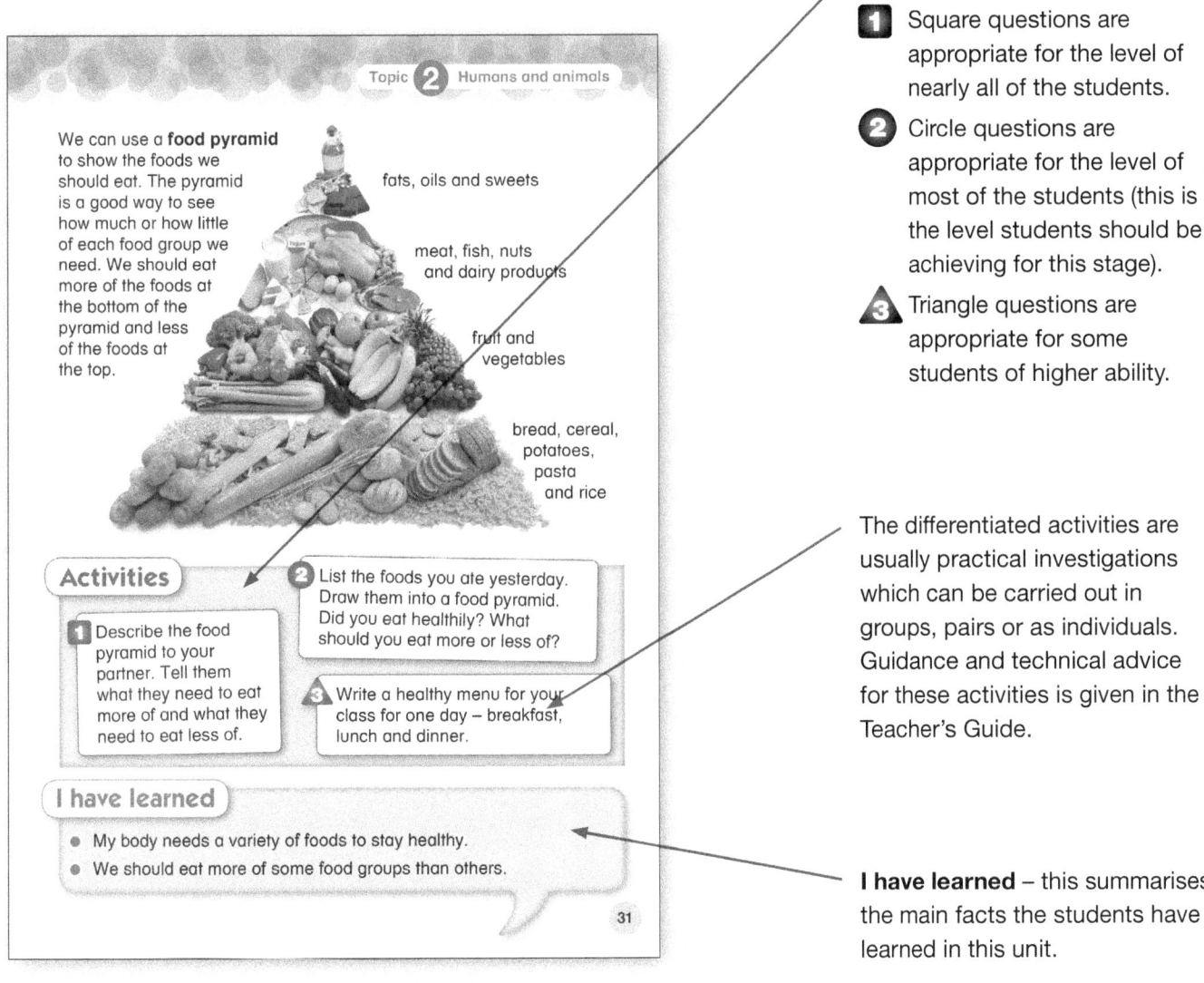

Activities

1 Square questions are appropriate for the level of nearly all of the students.

2 Circle questions are appropriate for the level of most of the students (this is the level students should be achieving for this stage).

3 Triangle questions are appropriate for some students of higher ability.

The differentiated activities are usually practical investigations which can be carried out in groups, pairs or as individuals. Guidance and technical advice for these activities is given in the Teacher's Guide.

I have learned – this summarises the main facts the students have learned in this unit.

At the back of the Student's Book is a comprehensive **Glossary** of all the Key words that are used during the lessons.

Workbook

The Workbook is for students to record observations, investigation results and key learning during the lesson. It has structured spaces for the students to record work and guidance on what to do. It gives the teacher an opportunity to give the student written feedback and becomes part of each student's work portfolio.

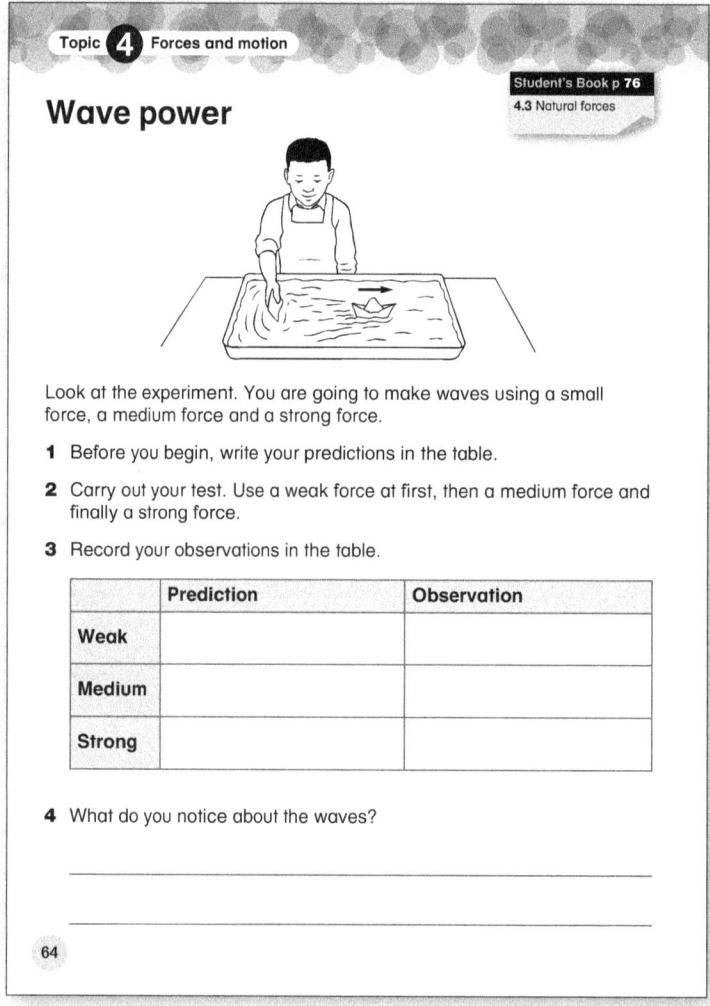

DVD

The DVD provides teachers with a set of electronic resources to support learning and assessment. The lesson plans in this Teacher's Guide give references in the *Resources* box and in the body of text to the relevant video clips, slideshows and interactive 'drag and drop' activities.

Interactive 'drag and drop' activities

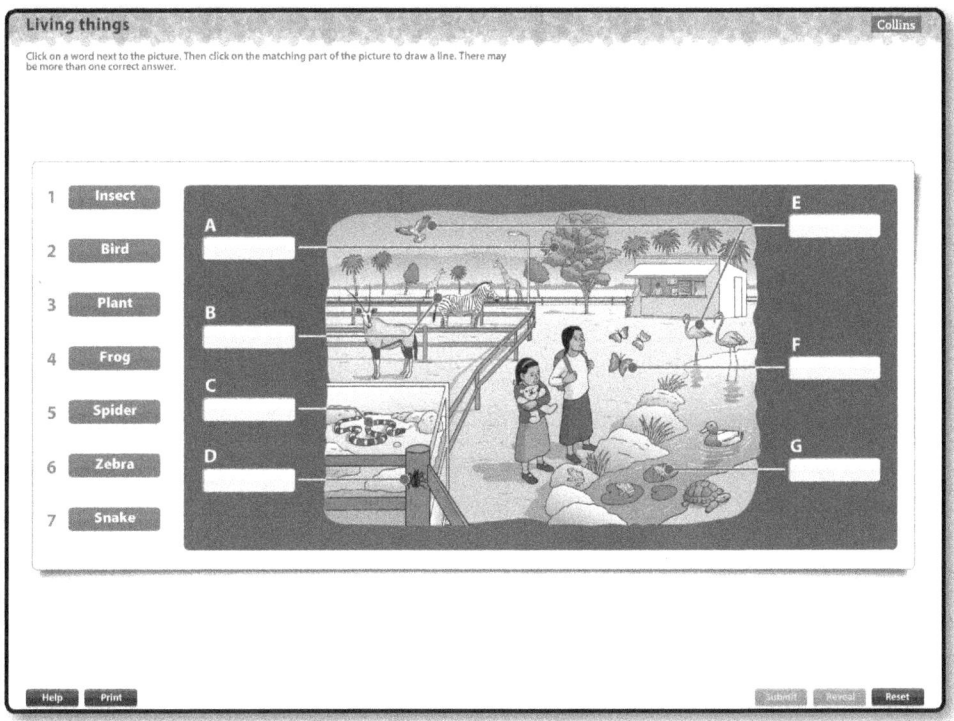

Slideshows and video clips

Assessment in primary science

In the primary science programme, assessment is a continuous, planned process that involves collecting information about student progress and learning in order to provide constructive feedback to students and parents, but also to inform planning and the next teaching steps.

Cambridge Assessment International Education Primary curriculum framework for science makes it clear what the students are expected to learn and achieve at each level. Our task as teachers is to make sure that we assess whether (or not) the students have achieved the stated goals using clearly-focused, varied, reliable and flexible methods of assessment.

In the Collins Primary Science course, assessment is continuous and in-built. It applies the principles of international best practice and ensures that assessment:

- is ongoing and regular
- supports individual achievement and allows for the students to reflect on their learning and set targets for themselves
- provides feedback and encouragement to the students
- allows for the integration of assessment into activities and classroom teaching by combining different assessment methods, including observations, questioning, self-assessment, formal and informal tasks
- uses strategies that cater for the variety of student needs in the classroom (language, physical, emotional and cultural), and acknowledges that the students do not all need to be assessed at the same time or in the same way
- allows for more formal summative assessment including controlled activities, tasks and class tests.

Assessing scientific enquiry skills

The development of scientific enquiry skills needs to be monitored. You need to check that the students acquire the basic skills as you teach and make sure that they are able to apply them in more complex activities and situations later on.

You can do this by identifying the assessment opportunities in different enquiry-based tasks and by asking appropriate informal assessment questions as the students work through and complete the tasks.

For example, the students may be involved in an activity where they are expected to plan and carry out a fair test investigating cars and ramps (*Plan investigative work:* Recognise that a test or comparison may be unfair).

As the students work through the activity you have the opportunity to assess whether they are able to identify:

- one thing that will change
- what things they will measure and record
- what things will be kept the same.

Once they have completed the task, you can ask some informal assessment questions, such as:

- Is a test the only way to do a scientific investigation? (*No, there are other methods of collecting and recording information, including using secondary sources.*)
- Is every test a fair test?
- Are there special things we need to do to make sure a test is fair?
- What should we do before we can carry out a fair test properly? (*Develop and write up a plan.*)
- Is a fair test in science the same as a written science or maths test at school?
- How is it different?

Assessment in primary science

Formal written assessment

The Collins Primary Science course offers a selection of Assessment Sheets that teachers can use to formally assess learning and to award marks if necessary. These sheets include questions posed in different ways, questions where the students fill in answers or draw diagrams and true or false questions, among others.

Below are some examples of the types of questions provided on the Assessment Sheets.

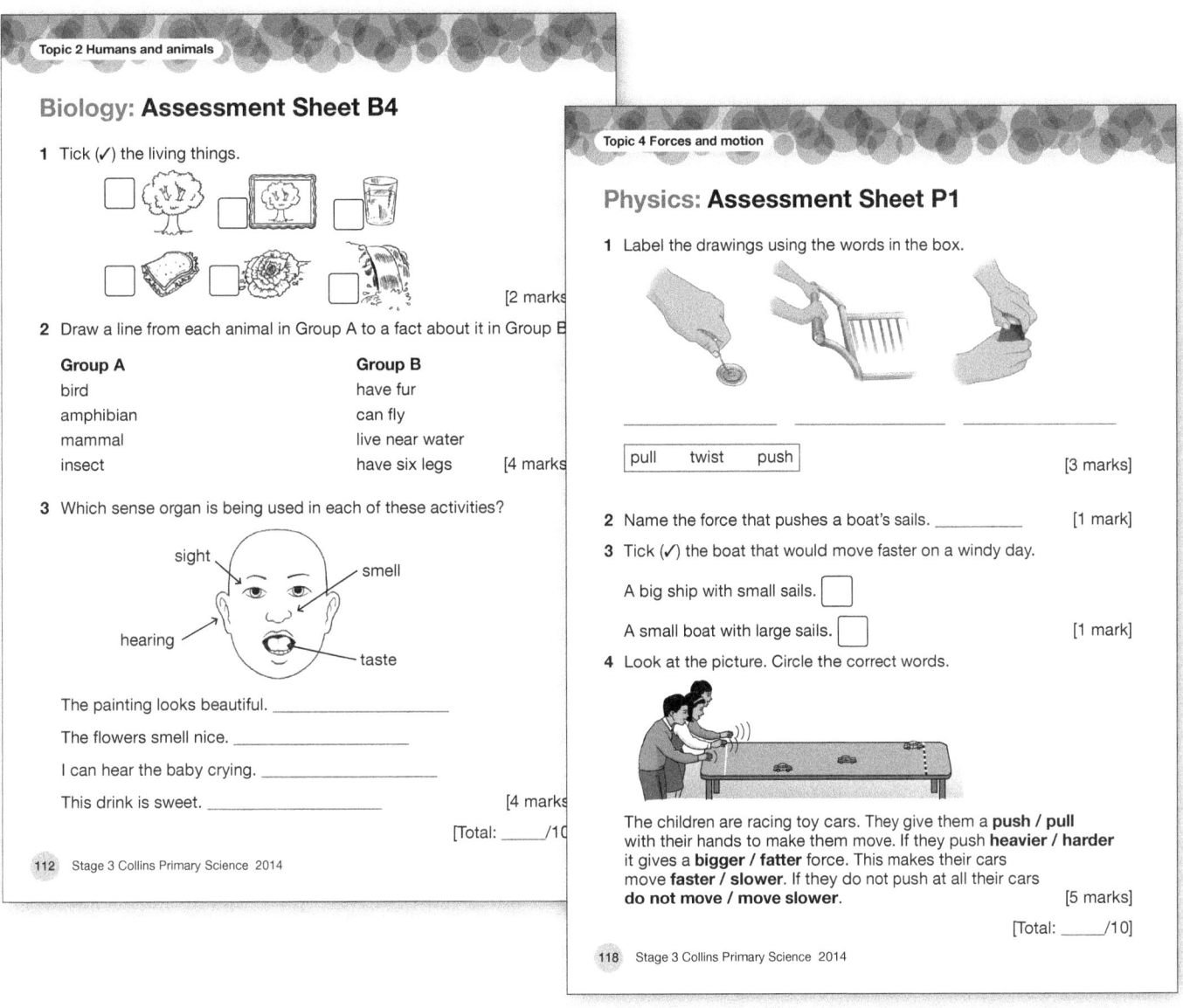

In addition to the materials supplied in the course, schools may opt for their students to take standardised CIE progression tests at Stages 3, 4, 5 and 6. These tests are developed by Cambridge but they are written and marked in schools. Teachers download the tests and administer them in their own classrooms. Cambridge Assessment International Education provides a mark scheme and you can upload learners' test results and then analyse the results and create and print reports. You can also compare a learner's results against their class, school or other schools around the world and on a year-by-year basis.

Learning objectives matching grid

Stage 3 Biology Learning Objectives	Topic	Unit	Teacher's Guide pages
Plants			
Know that plants have roots, leaves, stems and flowers.	1	1	2
	1	2	4
	1	10	20
	1	Consolidation	22
Explain observations that plants need water and light to grow.	1	3	6
	1	4	8
	1	Consolidation	22
Know that water is taken in through the roots and transported through the stem.	1	2	4
	1	Consolidation	22
Know that plants need healthy roots, leaves and stems to grow well.	1	6	12
	1	Consolidation	22
Know that plant growth is affected by temperature.	1	5	10
	1	7	14
	1	8	16
	1	9	18
	1	Consolidation	22
Humans and animals			
Know life processes common to humans and animals include nutrition (water and food), movement, growth and reproduction.	2	1	24
	2	Consolidation	44
Describe differences between living and non-living things using knowledge of life processes.	2	2	26
	2	Consolidation	44
Explore and research exercise and the adequate, varied diet needed to keep healthy.	2	3	28
	2	4	30
	2	6	34
	2	Consolidation	44
Know that some foods can be damaging to health, e.g. very sweet and fatty foods.	2	5	32
	2	Consolidation	44
Explore human senses and the ways we use them to learn about our world.	2	7	36
	2	8	38
	2	Consolidation	44
Sort living things into groups, using simple features and describe rationale for groupings.	2	9	40
	2	10	42
	2	Consolidation	44

Learning objectives matching grid

Stage 3 Chemistry Learning Objectives	Topic	Unit	Teacher's Guide pages
Material properties			
Know that every material has specific properties, e.g. hard, soft, shiny.	3	1	46
	3	2	48
	3	3	50
	3	4	52
	3	5	54
	3	7	58
	3	8	60
	3	9	62
	3	10	64
	3	Consolidation	70
Sort materials according to their properties.	3	1	46
	3	2	48
	3	3	50
	3	4	52
	3	7	58
	3	8	60
	3	9	62
	3	10	64
	3	Consolidation	70
Explore how some materials are magnetic but many are not.	3	11	66
	3	12	68
	3	Consolidation	70
Discuss why materials are chosen for specific purposes on the basis of their properties.	3	3	50
	3	4	52
	3	5	54
	3	6	56
	3	7	58
	3	9	62
	3	10	64
	3	12	68
	3	Consolidation	70

Stage 3 Physics Learning Objectives	Topic	Unit	Teacher's Guide pages
Forces and motion			
Know that pushes and pulls are examples of forces and that they can be measured with forcemeters.	4	1	72
	4	4	78
	4	Consolidation	88
Explore how forces can make objects start or stop moving.	4	2	74
	4	3	76
	4	5	80
	4	Consolidation	88
Explore how forces can change the shape of objects.	4	7	84
	4	Consolidation	88
Explore how forces, including friction, can make objects move faster or slower or change direction.	4	6	82
	4	8	86
	4	Consolidation	88

Scientific enquiry skills matching grid

Stage 3 Scientific enquiry skills	Topic	Unit	Teacher's Guide page
Ideas and evidence			
Collect evidence in a variety of contexts to answer questions or test ideas.	1	4	8
	1	6	12
	1	7	14
	2	1	24
	2	2	26
	2	4	30
	2	6	34
	2	7	36
	3	1	46
	3	2	48
	3	3	50
	3	4	52
	3	5	54
	3	7	58
	3	8	60
	3	11	66
	4	1	72
	4	2	74
	4	3	76
	4	4	78
	4	5	80
	4	6	82
	4	7	84
	4	8	86

Stage 3 Scientific enquiry skills	Topic	Unit	Teacher's Guide page
Plan investigative work			
Suggest ideas, make predictions and communicate these.	1	2	4
	1	3	6
	1	4	8
	1	5	10
	1	8	16
	2	5	32
	2	6	34
	2	8	38
	3	1	46
	3	3	50
	3	4	52
	3	5	54
	3	6	56
	3	7	58
	3	8	60
	3	9	62
	3	10	64
	3	11	66
	3	12	68
	4	1	72
	4	2	74
	4	3	76
	4	4	78
	4	5	80
	4	6	82
	4	8	86
With help, think about collecting evidence and planning fair tests.	1	3	6
	1	4	8
	1	6	12
	2	7	36
	3	2	48
	3	3	50
	3	7	58
	3	10	64
	4	2	74
	4	3	76
	4	5	80

Scientific enquiry skills matching grid

Stage 3 Scientific enquiry skills	Topic	Unit	Teacher's Guide page
Obtain and present evidence			
Observe and compare objects, living things and events.	1	1	2
	1	2	4
	1	5	10
	1	7	14
	1	8	16
	1	9	18
	1	10	20
	2	1	24
	2	4	30
	2	5	32
	2	8	38
	2	9	40
	2	10	42
	3	1	46
	3	2	48
	3	4	52
	3	5	54
	3	6	56
	3	7	58
	3	8	60
	3	9	62
	3	10	64
	3	11	66
	3	12	68
	4	5	80
	4	6	82
Measure using simple equipment and record observations in a variety of ways.	2	6	34
	2	7	36
	3	3	50
	3	7	58
	3	8	60
	4	4	78
	4	7	84

Stage 3 Scientific enquiry skills	Topic	Unit	Teacher's Guide page
Present results in drawings, bar charts and tables.	1	3	6
	1	4	8
	1	6	12
	1	7	14
	1	10	20
	2	1	24
	2	3	28
	2	4	30
	2	5	32
	3	3	50
	3	4	52
	4	5	80
	4	8	86
Consider evidence and approach			
Draw conclusions from results and begin to use scientific knowledge to suggest explanations.	1	5	10
	1	9	18
	2	1	24
	2	6	34
	2	10	42
	3	2	48
	3	3	50
	3	8	60
	3	11	66
	3	12	68
	4	3	76
	4	4	78
	4	8	86
Make generalisations and begin to identify simple patterns in results.	1	6	12
	1	10	20
	2	2	26
	2	9	40
	3	2	48
	3	5	54
	3	11	66
	4	2	74
	4	5	80
	4	6	82

xvii

Lesson plans

Biology 2

Chemistry 40

Physics 54

Biology • Topic 1 Plants

1.1 Parts of plants

Student's Book pages 2–3
Biology learning objective
- Know that plants have roots, leaves, stems and flowers.

Resources
- Workbook pages 1 and 2
- Video B1: Plants in the sun and rain

Classroom equipment
- a healthy flowering pot plant or garden plant with plenty of leaves
- a collection of leaves of different sizes and shapes
- set of cards with the names and functions of plant parts written on (optional)

Scientific enquiry skills
- *Obtain and present evidence:* Observe and compare objects, living things and events.

Key words
- leaves
- stem
- roots
- flowers

⚠️ Students should avoid all poisonous plants and should check with an adult before they take samples of leaves to ensure that they are not poisonous. If you are in doubt, do not let them pick the leaf.

Scientific background

The main parts of almost all plants are the *roots*, *leaves*, *stems*, *flowers*, fruits and seeds.

The roots help provide support by anchoring the plant in the ground and absorbing water and nutrients needed for growth.

The leaves use energy from the Sun, carbon dioxide and water to make sugar (glucose) and oxygen. This process is called *photosynthesis*. Oxygen is given off as part of this process.

Stems carry water and nutrients taken up by the roots to the leaves. Food produced by the leaves is then transported to other parts of the plant. Stems also keep leaves clear of the ground and allow leaves to reach as much sunlight as possible.

Flowers are important in making seeds as they contain pollen, which combines with other parts of the flower to grow seeds. Petals are important parts of the flower because they help attract pollinators such as bees and butterflies which carry pollen from plant to plant to start the seed-forming process.

Introduction

- Review what the students already know about plants. They should be able to recognise and name the roots, stems, leaves and flowers of a plant.
- Show Video B1, of plants growing in the sunshine and the rain. Ask: *How does the video show that the plants are alive?* (They are moving and responding to the light.) *Which parts of the plant are moving? Why are the plants moving?*
- Show the class a healthy indoor pot plant or the plant that you have prepared for the lesson. It should have flowers and plenty of leaves, Ask: *Why do plants have lots of different parts?* (Because they all need to do different jobs to keep the plant alive.)
- Point to each of the different parts of the plant. For each part, ask students: *What is the name of this part? What job does it do?*

Biology • Topic 1 Plants 1.1

Teaching and learning activities

- Ask students to turn to page 2 of their Student's Books and to look at the labelled picture of the flowering plant. Read through the jobs that each part of the plant does with the students. You could ask for volunteers to read about each part. As students identify the parts and their jobs from the book, show them the same parts on your plant in the classroom.

- Talk about the questions with the class. Show the students that the plant takes in water from the ground and then trace the path of the water as it moves from the roots, through the stem, to the leaves and flowers. Ask what they think would happen if a plant couldn't get water.

- Ask students to do the activity on page 1 of their Workbooks. They should label the parts of a plant, and write down the job each part does.

- Take the class outside to collect leaves for the next part of the lesson. Remind students that they should ask an adult for permission and help when they are collecting their leaves. Stress that this is important as some plants are poisonous.

Graded activities

1 Ask the students to study photographs A and B on page 3 of the Student's Book. Tell the students that although the two plants are very different, they share common parts. Ask them to identify the roots, stems, leaves and flowers. If there are other plants in the classroom, extend the activity to include identifying the parts of these plants too.

2 The students should have collected at least five leaves each. These can be fallen leaves or leaves taken (with help and permission) from a live plant. In their groups, they should discuss the similarities and differences in their collections. Point out the veins and the leaf stalks to the students. Ask: *What do you think the purpose or job of the vein is? What connects the leaf to the rest of the plant?* After the discussion, ask students to complete the activity on page 2 of their Workbooks. They will draw and label two of the leaves from their collection.

3 Encourage the students to extend their knowledge. Ask: *What leaves can you eat? What leaves do you eat every day?* Ask them to make a list of edible leaves and mark which ones they eat regularly.

Consolidate and review

- Describe the function of a part of the plant and ask students to name the part. You could do a matching exercise with one set of cards labelled with plant names and another set of cards labelled with plant part functions. Alternatively, you could do this as a chalkboard exercise.

- Draw a leaf on the board and ask the students what part of a plant it is. Ask: *Which part of the leaf is the vein? Which is the leaf stalk?* Get students to check their drawings in their Workbooks to make sure that they have labelled their leaves correctly. Circulate while they are doing this and offer help where needed.

Differentiation

■ All of the students should know and be able to identify the different parts of a plant. They should all know that each part of the plant has a particular function.

● Most of the students should be able to give the function of each part of the plant and know that although plants are different and look different, they all have the same parts, performing the same function.

▲ Some of the students should be able to identify things that are common in leaves and make a list of edible leaves.

Biology • Topic 1 Plants 1.2

1.2 Plant roots and stems

Student's Book pages 4–5

Biology learning objectives
- Know that plants have roots, leaves, stems and flowers.
- Know that water is taken in through the roots and transported through the stem.

Resources
- Workbook pages 3 and 4

Classroom equipment
- edible leaves – lettuce, cabbage, parsley etc.
- a weed that shows all the parts of a plant
- coloured pens or pencils
- slice through a tree trunk showing annual rings (optional)
- a selection of root vegetables – carrots, beetroot etc.
- bean seeds and cotton wool (optional)

Scientific enquiry skills
- *Plan investigative work:* Suggest ideas, make predictions and communicate these.
- *Obtain and present evidence:* Observe and compare objects, living things and events.

Key words
- tap root
- fibrous root
- weed
- tree
- trunk

⚠️ Students must ask permission to dig up any plants, especially weeds. They should check with an adult that the plant or weed is not poisonous. If you are unsure, do not let them dig it up.

Scientific background

Plants use their roots to hold them in the soil. The roots provide support by anchoring the plant and absorbing water and nutrients that the plant needs to grow.

Some roots go a long way down into the soil. These are called *tap roots*. Other roots spread out widely to use the water all around them. They are called *fibrous roots*. The roots of some plants become very fat, because the plant stores food, in form of sugars and carbohydrates, in them. The Cambridge Primary Science framework does not specify that the students need to be able to differentiate between tap, fibrous and storage roots. This activity has been included here for enrichment purposes and for additional information only.

Stems carry water and nutrients taken up by the roots to the leaves and flowers. The leaves then use the water and nutrients with sunlight to make food. This process is called *photosynthesis*. Stems also provide support for the plant, allowing the leaves to reach the sunlight they need to produce food.

Trees are plants too. The stem of a tree is called a *trunk*. As trees get older, their trunks get thicker. You can tell how old a tree is by counting the number of rings inside its trunk. Every year a new ring forms. These rings are called *annual* rings (yearly rings).

Introduction

- Show the class the collection of edible leaves you have brought in. Ask: *What kind of leaf is this?* (Cabbage, lettuce, parsley etc.) Ask: *Who eats leaves like this at home?* Ask students to share their list of edible leaves with the rest of the class. Make a list on the board as students volunteer their answers. Discuss the common features of the leaves. If students ask, name the midrib (the central line down the leaf), veins (the branches off the midrib) and the blade (the flat part of the leaf). Ask: *Which leaf is your favourite?* Ask students to talk about when these leaves are eaten in their homes.

Teaching and learning activities

- Hold up the *weed* you have dug up. Ask the class to identify the different parts. Talk about the roots. What shape are they? Does the plant have one long tap root, or does it have lots of fibrous roots, which spread out widely? Ask: *Why would a plant need a tap root?* (To get to water deep in the ground.)

- Ask: *Why would a plant need fibrous roots?* (To gather water at the surface.)
- Now discuss the stem of your plant. Ask: *What does a stem do? Where does it transport the water? Why do the leaves need the water?*
- Turn to the Student's Book and discuss the pictures and questions on page 4. Talk about the role of roots in more detail. Explain the difference between the three root systems shown. Ask students to say which is a tap root, which is a fibrous root and which is a root that is storing food. Ask: *What is the name of the root that is storing food?* (Carrot.)
- Ask students to discuss in groups where we could find the different roots. Circulate while they are doing this, offering assistance where necessary.

Graded activities

1 Ask the students to dig up a weed, taking care not to break the roots (they can either do this in the school grounds or bring in a weed from home). The students should draw and label their weed on page 3 of their Workbooks. Circulate while they are drawing and offer assistance where necessary. Make sure that the labels for the different parts are correct. You may want to write the names of the parts on the board for easy reference.

2 In their groups, the students should discuss and draw the root vegetables that they eat regularly. You can assist them in their discussions by giving examples such as carrots, beetroot etc. Note that a potato is not a swollen root – it is actually a tuber, which grows off the root. You can accept it as a root vegetable at this stage, but alert the students to the fact that it is a special case.

3 Discuss the fact that trees are plants too and that their stems are called trunks. Talk about the way you can tell the age of a tree and, if possible, demonstrate a tree trunk with rings (slices of trunks are often sold at nurseries as natural paving or for use in gardens). The students should record the results of the tree survey on page 4 of their Workbooks. They should draw a tree from the playground or one that grows near their home, and then fill in the information required.

Ask a few students to share the results of their tree survey. How many students in the class chose the same kind of tree? What was common about the information gathered? Did anyone choose an unusual tree? Ask them to tell the class about it.

Consolidate and review

- Show the students your selection of root vegetables. Ask: *What is the role of each of these roots for the plant?* Students should be able to say that they are storing food and some may also say that they are holding the plant in the soil.
- Discuss what would happen if plants were missing any of their parts. Ask: *What would happen if a plant didn't have a stem? Could a plant survive without roots?* The idea is to emphasise the importance of each part of the plant and its role.
- You could encourage students to grow their own plants, so that they can observe for themselves how necessary each part is. Perhaps you could do this as a class activity, with each student growing a bean in damp cotton wool. It would be easy then to see that the stem and root develop from the seed. You will need three plants later, for activities in Units 1.3 and 1.4.

Differentiation

■ All of the students should know that plant roots hold the plant in the soil and that they take in water. They should know that the stem supports the plant and carries the water to other parts of the plant.

● Most of the students should be able to explain the different kinds of root structures and their functions.

▲ Some of the students should be able to explain why plants have different root structures and they will understand that different root structures are needed in different environments.

Big Cat

Students who have read *Big Cat The oak tree* will have been introduced to the parts of the tree, including the roots, trunk, branches and leaves, and will have a good grounding in this topic already.

Biology • Topic 1 Plants 1.3

1.3 Plants need water

Student's Book pages 6–7

Biology learning objective
- Explain observations that plants need water and light to grow.

Resources
- Workbook pages 5 and 6

Classroom equipment
- the same pot plant or garden plant as in Unit 1.1, unwatered since that lesson
- Three bean plants per pair of students. Students can use the bean plants that they may have planted in Unit 1.2.
- coloured pens or pencils
- rulers

Scientific enquiry skills
- *Plan investigative work:* Suggest ideas, make predictions and communicate these; with help, think about collecting evidence and planning fair tests.
- *Obtain and present evidence:* Present results in drawings, bar charts and tables.

Key words
- **minerals**
- **absorb**
- **transport**

Scientific background

Roots anchor the plant in the ground and *absorb* the water and nutrients (or *minerals*) that plants need for growth. Water is absorbed through the roots and *transported* to the leaves through the stem. Wherever they live, plants need water to survive – just like all living things. Without water, plants will shrivel up and die.

Introduction

- Begin the lesson by encouraging students to look at the pot plant you showed them in Unit 1.1. Ask them if they can see any differences in it between now and before. What do they think causes the differences? Ask a student to water the plant.
- Talk about the other things that plants need to grow. Say: *You have just given the plant some water. What would happen if you did not water a plant?* Accept answers like: it would shrivel up, it would go brown or it would die.

Teaching and learning activities

- Turn to page 6 of the Student's Book. Talk about the two photographs, which show very different plants. Get students to identify the plants. Ask them what is the same and what is different about the plants. Answers may include: size, colour, where they store their extra food, that one has a very long stem (trunk) and the other a very short stem, etc. Ask the students to name each part of the two plants.
- Encourage students to work in pairs and discuss the questions. Circulate while they are talking and assist where necessary. Students may guess that the palm tree has a tap root to anchor it and the cabbage has shallow branch roots, as it is a much smaller plant and does not need as deep an anchor as the tree.
- Ask the students to turn to page 5 of their Workbooks. Instruct them to use a coloured pencil to show the path of water through the plant. They should draw arrows to show the direction in which the water moves. Make sure the students label all the parts through which the water moves.

Biology • Topic 1 Plants 1.3

Graded activities

As this is a practical investigation, it is recommended that the students work in mixed ability groups for this activity. Differentiation should be through the level of support the students receive as they work on the activity, as well as by outcome (please see guidance in the 'Differentiation' box right).

1 Show the class your three plants. The focus in this activity is on showing students the way to set up a fair test. This is a guided activity – in the next unit students will be planning their own investigation and making sure it is fair. Ask: *What do plants need to grow?* Write the students' answers on the board. Respond to the students' suggestions. Say: *Let's start by investigating one thing that plants need to grow: water.*

2 Students can use the bean plants that they may have planted in Unit 1.2. While the pairs or groups are working, circulate and check that all the plants are being placed in areas where they get exactly the same amount of sunlight. For those who are confused, explain that the only thing you want to change is the amount of water the plants receive and that everything else needs to be kept the same to ensure the test is fair.

3 Students should record the results of their fair test on page 6 of their Workbooks at the end of week 1 and week 2. It is very important that they begin their test by writing down the condition of the plants at the start. So make sure they measure their plants and record their height and that they write a full description of the colour and size of each plant.

Consolidate and review

- Review students' predictions from the beginning of the lesson. Ask for a show of hands. How many students think the plant that is not going to get water will die? Which plant do they think is going to be the healthiest at the end of two weeks? Ask: *Is there such a thing as too much water? What would happen to a plant that received too much water?*

- If you have time, you can instruct the class to draw the three plants in their exercise books. They should label each part. This is good revision and good practice at scientific record-keeping.

Differentiation

■ All of the students should be able to explain where and how plants get their water. They should be able to predict what will happen if a plant does not receive any water.

● Most of the students should be able to set up an investigation to see what will happen if a plant is deprived of water.

▲ Some of the students should be able to explain why it is important to make an investigation a fair test and ways in which they made this particular investigation a fair test.

Biology • Topic 1 Plants 1.4

1.4 Plants need sunlight

Student's Book pages 8–9

Biology learning objective
- Explain observations that plants need water and light to grow.

Resources
- Workbook pages 7 and 8
- Video B2: Plants grow towards sunlight
- Video B3: What plants need
- PCM B1: Planning an investigation
- PCM B2: Shoebox maze

Classroom equipment
- three healthy bean plants
- ruler
- coloured pens or pencils
- a prepared shoebox maze (see instructions on PCM B2)

Scientific enquiry skills
- *Ideas and evidence:* Collect evidence in a variety of contexts to answer questions or test ideas.
- *Plan investigative work:* Suggest ideas, make predictions and communicate these; with help, think about collecting evidence and planning fair tests.
- *Obtain and present evidence:* Present results in drawings, bar graphs and tables.

Key words
- energy
- carbon dioxide

Scientific background

Leaves are the food-making factories of the plant. They are made to catch sunlight, and have openings in them to allow water and air to come and go. The outer surfaces of leaves are covered by a waxy coating called a cuticle, which protects the leaves and prevents excessive water loss. Veins carry water and nutrients within the leaves.

Plants need sunlight to grow. They absorb energy *from* the sunlight through their leaves and combine it with water from the roots and *carbon dioxide* from the air to make food, in a process called photosynthesis. This food is stored as sugar (glucose). In the process oxygen is given off. The plant uses the sugar to grow.

Introduction

- Start the lesson by asking students to imagine what the world would be like without any plants. You may get a range of answers from 'It would look plain' to 'There would be no oxygen to breathe' depending on the students' prior knowledge of the function of plants and the process of photosynthesis. Ask: *Where do we get our food from? Where do animals get their food from?* Help the class to realise that plants are very special, because they make their own food, and that this makes them different from other living things. Direct students to the photographs on page 10 of the Student's Book and ask where the living things in the photographs get their food from.
- Talk briefly about the leaves of the plant and explain that the leaves are the food-making factory of the plant. You can introduce the term 'photosynthesis', but do not go into too much detail. Ask: *What's the main job of the leaves of a plant? What part does sunlight play in this?*

Teaching and learning activities

- Students now work in pairs to use what they learned in the previous unit. They should discuss their test first, then plan how to make it a fair test. Students should use PCM B2 to help them plan their investigation. Depending on the context in which you teach, you may want to do this as group work instead of pair work. If so, assign each member of the group a role.

Biology • Topic 1 Plants 1.4

◆ Show Video B2 (plants growing towards sunlight) and ask the students to describe what is happening. Tell the students again that plants use energy from the sunlight, plus water and carbon dioxide from the air to make sugars in the leaves. The plant then uses these sugars for energy to grow.

◆ Ask students what you could do to test whether plants need sunlight to grow. Accept different answers, then narrow it down to putting one plant in direct sunlight on a windowsill and another plant in a dark cupboard and observing what happens after a week.

● Talk about ways in which you could make sure this is a fair test. Ask: *Which plant will grow the best? How will you judge how healthy each plant is?* Build up a list on the board of health-checks for plants: good colour of leaves, plant not droopy, firm stem etc. Explain that to keep a test fair, you need to keep all the conditions the same, except for the one you are testing. Ask: *Would it be a fair test if we gave the two plants differing amounts of water?* (No, it would not be a fair test, as they need the same amount of water.)

Graded activities

As this is a practical investigation, it is recommended that the students work in mixed ability groups for this activity. Differentiation should be through the level of support the students receive as they work on the activity, as well as by outcome (please see guidance in the 'Differentiation' box right).

1 Students prepare and set up the experiment. You could ask them to keep a daily note of what is happening to their plants if you see the cupboard plant drooping more quickly than anticipated.

2 Students need to check the plants every day and then record the results in the table on page 7 of their Workbooks at the end of the week. They should write down the colour and height of both plants and draw the plants in their Workbooks on page 8.

3 Get the students to write an explanation of ways to ensure a fair test in their exercise books. Circulate and check that everyone has grasped this concept.

Consolidate and review

● Show the class the prepared maze box (see PCM B2). Ask: *What will happen if we put the third plant in the maze box?* Put the box in a sunny position and water the plant. Ask students to predict what will happen to the plant.

● Show the students Video B3 about what plants need to grow healthily, to consolidate what they have learned.

Differentiation

■ All of the students should be able to state one thing that must be kept the same in a fair test, for example, the amount of water.

● Most of the students should be able to describe ways to control variables, for example, light, water, heat, soil, type of plant.

▲ Some of the students should be able to explain why it is important to make an experiment a fair test.

Biology • Topic 1 Plants 1.5

1.5 Plants need warmth

Student's Book pages 10–11

Biology learning objective
- Know that plant growth is affected by temperature.

Resources
- Workbook page 9
- PCM B3: Plants in the environment

Classroom equipment
- beans for sprouting (e.g. cress, mung beans, lentils, chick peas etc.), glass jars, cheesecloth
- For each pair of students: cotton wool and saucers, beans, water, access to a warm place, like a windowsill and a cool place, like a fridge,

Scientific enquiry skills
- *Plan investigative work:* Suggest ideas, make predictions and communicate these.
- *Obtain and present evidence:* Observe and compare objects, living things and events.
- *Consider evidence and approach:* Draw conclusions from results and begin to use scientific knowledge to suggest explanations.

Key words
- **warmth**
- **temperature**

Scientific background

Plants only grow well in the right conditions. *Temperatures* that are too hot or too cold affect plant growth. The main source of *warmth* for plants is the Sun. In spring, the warmth from the Sun raises the temperature of both the air and the soil and seeds that have lain dormant throughout winter begin to germinate.

Seeds germinate in warm conditions and can lie dormant for years until the environment is right for germination.

Introduction

- Begin the lesson by encouraging students to look at their investigation from Unit 1.3. Ask: *Which plant is doing best? Which plant is drooping?* Let them record their observations on page 6 of their Workbooks.
- Now ask the students to check their investigation from Unit 1.4 and make notes about the plant on the windowsill and the one in the cupboard. Do they notice any differences? What do they think causes the differences? Get students to water their plants. Make sure they give each plant the same amount of water, so that the test they are conducting is fair.
- Establish that everyone understands that plants need water and sunlight to grow.

Teaching and learning activities

- Ask: *What else does a plant need to grow?* Accept answers such as fertiliser, nutrients etc. but lead the discussion towards 'warmth'. Ask: *When do most plants start to grow? What is different about this time of the year?* Explain that in spring the warmth from the Sun raises the temperature of the air and the soil, and that plants, especially seeds, need this warmth to grow.
- Ask the students to turn to page 10 of the Student's Book. Let them discuss the experiment. Point out all of the things which the children are doing that are the same (wetting the cotton wool, adding the bean seed, covering the seed etc.) Then ask the students to identify the things that are different.
- The students work in pairs to read and answer the questions on pages 10–11 of the Student's Book.

Biology • Topic **1** Plants 1.5

Graded activities

1 Students work in pairs to set up the investigation as shown in the pictures on page 10 of the Student's' Book. Circulate while this is happening, offering help where needed. Make sure that each pair of students is preparing identical saucers – the only difference must be the temperature to which the beans are exposed. Make sure that the students understand that this is necessary, as they are investigating the effect of temperature on plants and not the effect of light, which some students may be confused about.

2 Explain to the students that they are going to grow some seeds for their lunch! This can be done at home or in the classroom. You can write the instructions on the board, or read them out to the students as they work in pairs to follow your instructions. The seeds should be rinsed before the activity begins to remove impurities. Soak the seeds in water for 12 hours, in a jar, covered with cheesecloth. Place the jar in a warm place. After 12 hours, empty the jar by pouring the water through the cloth. Wash the seeds with cold water and place them back in the jar, in their warm place. Do this again 12 hours later. You should see a white root start to grow out of each seed. Tell the students that these seeds are now called 'bean sprouts'. You can eat the bean sprouts as they are or add them to a sandwich. They are very good for you.

3 The students should write a short paragraph about a seed that has been waiting for 10 000 years to grow. They should explain how they feel, as they begin to grow. Writing the paragraph requires the students to extend their thinking. Allow them to use their imagination, but make sure that they mention warmth, water and light as the three main impetuses for growth.

Consolidate and review

- Students should monitor the progress of their bean seeds over a week, and report back to the class about what is happening to their seeds, at least every second day. You can get the students to keep a written record of the two plants' growth in their exercise books.

Differentiation

■ All of the students should be able to say that plants need sunlight, water and warmth to grow. They will be able to set up their investigation with some help.

● Most of the students should be able to predict how temperature will affect a plant's growth. They should know that plants grow faster and better in a warm environment. They will follow the instructions carefully and successfully grow their own bean sprouts. If any students have a jar of beans that do not germinate use this as a discussion point to investigate why the bean sprouts may not have grown.

▲ Some of the students should be able to extend their knowledge and write an original paragraph about being a 10 000 year old plant that begins to germinate. They will make reference to warmth, light and water without being prompted.

Biology • Topic 1 Plants 1.6

1.6 Healthy plants

Student's Book pages 12–13

Biology learning objective
- Know that plants need healthy roots, leaves and stems to grow well.

Resources
- Workbook page 10 and 11
- Slideshow B1: Desert transformation
- DVD Activity B1: What plants need

Classroom equipment
- a bucket
- grass clippings
- vegetable peelings
- egg shells
- coffee grounds
- stick for stirring

Scientific enquiry skills
- *Ideas and evidence:* Collect evidence in a variety of contexts to answer questions or test ideas.
- *Plan investigative work:* With help, think about collecting evidence and planning fair tests.
- *Obtain and present evidence:* Present results in drawings, bar charts and tables.
- *Consider evidence and approach:* Make generalisations and begin to identify simple patterns in results.

Key words
- **fertiliser**
- **irrigate**

 Warn students to be careful when mixing the fertiliser. They should store it outside, in a place where it will not get in anyone's way or be knocked over accidentally.

Scientific background

Plants need healthy roots, stems and leaves to grow well. People can help plants to grow well by adding *fertiliser* to the soil and by *irrigating* the soil in dry areas.

Most fertilisers are based on the three major plant nutrients: nitrogen (N) for green leafy growth, phosphorus (P) for healthy root and shoot growth, and potassium (K) for flowering, fruiting and general hardiness. Fertilisers have different N:P:K ratios, depending on what they are used for.

Inorganic fertilisers are made using chemicals, whereas natural ones are not. Inorganic fertilisers are usually concentrated and fast-acting but because they are manufactured, a lot of energy is needed to make them, so they have a high carbon footprint. Organic fertilisers are made from dead plants and animals. They are much slower-acting, but have a much lower carbon footprint, so are more environmentally friendly.

Large-scale irrigation is only possible when there is a reliable fresh water source close to the area to be irrigated. In desert areas this can be tricky, but irrigation has been successful in areas of the UAE, Kuwait and Qatar.

The Cambridge Primary Science framework does not specify that the students need to have a knowledge of fertilisers or irrigation. This activity has been included here for enrichment purposes and for additional information only.

Introduction

- Remind the students of previous lessons in which they have grown plants. Ask: *What are the main requirements for plants to grow?* (They should include water, soil, sunlight, warmth and air.)
- Ask: *Why, if you irrigated the desert, would plants still not grow?* Discuss the fact that there are not enough nutrients in the soil to help the plant form proper roots, stems and leaves. Tell the students that if we ate only bread, we would not grow well because this food does not supply all the vitamins and minerals we need. In the same way, for plants to be healthy, they need a wide range of nutrients that they get from the soil. If the soil does not have these nutrients, we can add fertilisers to the soil to provide them.

Biology • Topic **1** Plants 1.6

Teaching and learning activities

- Ask the students to look at the pictures on page 12 of the Student's Book. They should discuss the questions in their groups and then write down the answers in their exercise books.
- Show Slideshow B1 (of arid desert land transformed into agricultural land by irrigation systems).
- Still in their groups, tell the students to imagine they are rich landowners and they have just bought a big piece of land on which they want to grow their crops. Each group should write a list of the things they should do to make sure that the land will produce good crops.
- Ask students to look at the picture on page 13 of the Student's Book. Encourage them to talk about what they can see. Use the questions as part of a whole-class discussion, encouraging the appropriate groups to offer answers.
- After the class discussion, get the students to work individually, writing the answers to the questions, in their own words, into their exercise books.
- Have a team debate on the topic. Ask: *Is it better to change desert land into agricultural land, or leave it as it is?* Make sure each member of the team has a chance to give his or her opinion, and that the debaters do not talk over each other. Stress that everyone has a valid opinion.

Graded activities

As this is a practical investigation the students should complete each step. Differentiation should be provided through the level of support the students are offered as they complete the activity, with some requiring prompting and others working independently.

1 Explain to students that they are going to make their own fertiliser. They need grass clippings or vegetable peelings, crushed egg shells, coffee grounds and water. Instruct them to mix this up in a bucket, and leave it outside in the sun for at least two weeks, giving it an occasional stir every few days. The finer the mixture, the easier the fertiliser will be to spread and use. You can do this as a class activity, or instruct the students to try this at home. Once the fertiliser mixture has been prepared and set aside, get the students to record what they did in their Workbooks on page 10.

2 Students should now plan a fair test to assess how good their fertiliser is and whether it will help plants to grow better. Remind them about the ways they planned a fair test in Units 1.3 and 1.4. What will they keep the same this time and what will they change?

3 Ask students to write down their fair test on page 11 of their Workbooks.

Consolidate and review

- Let the students complete DVD Activity B1 to consolidate what they have learned about the needs of plants.
- Make sure the students check on the progress of their two investigations and record the results. Ask if they think fertiliser would have improved the growth of their plants.

Differentiation

■ All of the students should be able to present at least one reason for changing the desert and one reason against.

● Most of the students should be able to present a balanced argument with at least three points for irrigating deserts and three points against.

▲ Some of the students should be able to use evidence to support their arguments.

Big Cat

Any students who have read *Big Cat Fragile Earth* may see connections between deserts and changes in climate.

Biology • Topic 1 Plants 1.7

1.7 Water plants

Student's Book pages 14–15
Biology learning objective
- Know that plant growth is affected by temperature.

Resources
- Workbook pages 12 and 13

Classroom equipment
- land and water plants for students to examine (pondweed is a good example of a plant that grows entirely underwater)
- coloured pens or pencils

Scientific enquiry skills
- *Ideas and evidence:* Collect evidence in a variety of contexts to answer questions or test ideas.
- *Obtain and present evidence:* Observe and compare objects, living things and events; present results in drawings, bar charts and tables.

⚠ Remind the students to wash their hands after handling plant material and not to touch their skin or mouths while handling the materials.

Scientific background

Water plants are adapted to live and grow either wholly or partially in water. Some water plants have roots that anchor the plant in the mud or soil at the bottom of the pond or river. Some water plants float freely on the surface of the water with their roots unanchored.

Just like land plants, all water plants need sunlight for photosynthesis. They also absorb nutrients through their roots (either from the soil or from the water).

Students may confuse seaweeds with water plants. Explain to the students that seaweeds are in fact a type of algae.

Introduction

- Explain that water plants are slightly different to plants that live on land. However, they do share many similarities. Ask: *How do water plants make their food?* Explain that water plants need sunlight to make their food, just as land plants do. Some float on the surface of the water; some are anchored by their roots in the mud or soil at the bottom, with a long stem leading to the surface.
- Quickly review the parts of land plants with the students.
- Ask the students to discuss any similarities water plants have with the land plants they have studied so far.

Teaching and learning activities

- Give each group a water plant in a beaker and a complete land plant. Compare the roots, stems, leaves and flowers (if they have them). The students should conclude that the stems of the water plants are not as tough or strong as those of land plants. Water plants may also have thin delicate leaves or leaves that float. Some water plants may have big roots, similar to those of land plants. Ask: *What do the plants feel like when you touch them? What do they smell like?*
- Talk about why water plants are different to land plants. Try to help students to the conclusion that they do not have to be as strong, because the water supports and protects them.
- Ask each group to give feedback on their ideas and allow groups to comment on each other's conclusions.

Biology • Topic 1 — Plants 1.7

Graded activities

1 Students work individually to complete this activity on page 12 of their Workbook. They should draw four different water plants on the section through the pond. The first should have roots that are growing in the mud at the bottom of the pond and leaves that grow upright out of the water (e.g. reeds) and the second have roots growing in the mud at the bottom of the pond and the leaves and flowers on the surface of the water (e.g. water lily). The third should have roots growing in the mud but its leaves and stem should be completely underwater (e.g pondweed) and the fourth should be floating on the water with roots that are not anchored in the soil (e.g duckweed).

2 The students should choose one land plant and one water plant and fill in the table on page 13 of their Workbook, identifying the similarities between them. They will use the knowledge that they gained during the lesson and they can also undertake further research using books or the internet.

3 To see if students are able to apply their new knowledge, ask them to design their own water plant. Give the students freedom and encourage them to use their imagination. They must label each part of their plant and explain in what ways it is suited to live in water.

Consolidate and review

- Give students the opportunity to present their invented water plants to their classmates, and to explain the ways in which the plant is suited to live in water. You could have an informal competition and choose the top three plants for small prizes.

- If you have space in your classroom, mount a wall display of the invented water plants. You could back the display with a pond scene, so that each student can place their plant where it is best suited to grow.

Differentiation

■ All of the students should be able to draw four different types of water plant in the pond with little or no help.

● Most of the students should be able to write what the role of each part is and ways in which water plants are similar to and different from land plants.

▲ Some of the students should be able to design a water plant that has roots, a stem and leaves and explain that it will need sunlight in order to make food.

Big Cat

Students who have read *Big Cat Pond food* have been introduced to the fact that some animals and plants can live underwater. They may recall some of the animals and plants that make their homes in a pond.

15

Biology • Topic 1 • Plants 1.8

1.8 Plants in the desert

Student's Book pages 16–17

Biology learning objective
- Know that plant growth is affected by temperature.

Resources
- Workbook page 14
- Slideshow B2: Trees in hot habitats
- PCM B4: Matching plant adaptations to habitats

Classroom equipment
- cactuses
- examples of products with aloe in them (if available)
- coloured pens or pencils

Scientific enquiry skills
- *Plan investigative work:* Suggest ideas, make predictions and communicate these.
- *Obtain and present evidence:* Observe and compare objects, living things and events.

Key words
- cactus
- spine
- sap

 Remind students to take care if handling cactuses.

Scientific background

Plants such as *cacti*, which can store water in their thick and fleshy leaves and stems, are succulents. Cactuses have sharp *spines* instead of leaves, so photosynthesis takes place in the plant's skin, which is also the stem. The stem has the ability to swell as it collects water, and then slowly contracts (shrinks) as the water is used by the plant.

Cactus spines, which are highly adapted leaves, protect the plant from animals and also allow night-time moisture to condense on them and drop to the ground, to be absorbed by the shallow roots. Some desert plants store water in a substance called *sap*. Aloe is a type of sap that has medicinal use for burns and scratches.

Although adaptation is not taught until Stage 4, the students should still be able to suggest reasons why some plants are more suited to growing in certain places than in others.

Introduction

- Ask the class to describe what conditions are like in the desert. Focus on previous learning about plants needing water to survive and stress how little rain there is in the desert. Ask: *What do plants need to survive?* (water, air and sunlight)

- Ask: *How do plants survive in the desert?* Let the students discuss this in their groups. Take feedback and write students' ideas on the board.

- Show students a growing cactus and ask individuals to describe it. Remove it from the pot, taking care when handling it, and show the students the roots. Remind the students about the role of the roots. Ask: *Do cactuses have flowers? Why are cactuses green? Where are the leaves on a cactus?* (The leaves are adapted into spines, which the plant uses as protection against animals, to stop the animals from eating it. The stem functions as the leaves and photosynthesis occurs in the stem).

Biology • Topic 1 Plants 1.8

Teaching and learning activities

- Ask the students to look at pages 16 and 17 of the Student's Book and to take turns to describe one of the plants to their partner.
- Stress that the ghaf tree has very long roots, which reach water far below the surface of the ground. Explain that deserts often have water very deep underground. Emphasise that cactuses and succulents store water to use when it is very dry: the cactus in its stem, and the aloe in its leaves. Show Slideshow B2, which is about trees in hot habitats.
- Give each pair of students a set of cards cut from PCM B4 and ask them to match the plants to the habitats.
- Let the students work in pairs to answer the questions. Circulate while students are discussing this, and assist or ask questions as necessary.

Graded activities

1. Students write out a list of desert plants that they know. Once everyone has finished, write a list of the plants up on your board for students to see.

2. In pairs, students fill in a table listing the names of three desert plants they have learned about, and how and where that plant stores water. Take feedback orally and get pairs to peer assess each other.

3. Ask the students to do some research. They must find out about another plant that is adapted to grow in very dry conditions. They should make a short presentation to the rest of the group saying what they have found out about their plant.

Consolidate and review

- The students should complete the activity on page 14 of their Workbook. They draw and write a description of a desert landscape, and the plants that are adapted to live there.
- Take feedback from students about the new plant they researched, which is adapted to live in very dry conditions. Make a table on the board, like the ones the students have in their books, and write down the names of the new plants and where and how they store water. Encourage the students to show pictures of their plants to their classmates.
- Ask students to look around them at plants that grow in your local conditions. In what ways are the plants in your area adapted to suit the weather and climate that you have? Discuss this as a whole-class activity.

Differentiation

■ All of the students should be able to explain that plants are adapted to suit their environment, whether it is a water environment or a desert.

● Most of the students will be able to give examples of ways in which plants are adapted to suit hot and dry conditions.

▲ Some of the students should be able to apply their knowledge of plant adaptations to the plants that grow in their own environment, and should be able to recognise local adaptations.

Biology • Topic 1 Plants 1.9

1.9 Mountain plants

Student's Book pages 18–19

Biology learning objective
- Know that plant growth is affected by temperature.

Resources
- Workbook page 15

Classroom equipment
- photos of alpine scenes, showing the snowline and pine or fir trees
- coloured pens or pencils
- if possible, samples of bark and needles from pine or fir trees

Scientific enquiry skills
- *Obtain and present evidence:* Observe and compare objects, living things and events.
- *Consider evidence and approach:* Draw conclusions from results and begin to use scientific knowledge to suggest explanations.

Key words
- alpine
- needle

Scientific background

Wherever they live, plants need water, air and sunlight. They are adapted to meet these needs within their habitat. *Alpine* plants are low-growing, to provide protection from strong winds, which often blow on mountains. Their leaves are tough and the roots form a network of short roots to anchor them well to the ground, and to collect what little water there may be between the rocks. Some plants have waxy leaves or tightly packed *needles* to limit evaporation or freezing from the windy and cold conditions.

Although adaptation is not taught until Stage 4, the students should still be able to suggest reasons why some plants are more suited to growing in certain places than in others.

Introduction

- Show the class the pictures of various alpine landscapes. Ask if anyone has been in snowy mountains. Get the students to share their own experiences. Ask: *What kinds of plants or trees grow in these very cold places?* Most students will come up with the answer: fir trees.
- Point out the snowline on the pictures to students. Explain that on most mountains this line marks the point that fir trees grow up to but not beyond. Explain that there are plants that grow above the snowline too. We call these *alpine plants*, from the word 'Alps'.

- Get students to suggest what sorts of plants would be suited to alpine conditions. Praise answers that mention ideas like 'low-growing', 'tough', 'small leaves', 'flowering only briefly', or 'very strong root system that burrows into cracks in rocks'.

Teaching and learning activities

- Let the students look at the picture on page 18 of the Student's Book. Ask them to describe the plants and their surroundings. Make sure that they realise that the plants are actually growing on very high mountains.
- Draw out that the alpine plant is adapted to its conditions by being low-growing. This protects it against the strong winds that often blow on mountains. It has a network of short roots that anchor it well to the ground and enable it to collect water from the shallow soil in rocky crevices.
- Let the students work in groups to discuss the questions. Then direct the students to the activity in their Workbooks on page 15. Students have to decide where to locate alpine plants, fir trees and water plants like algae in the environment in front of them.
- Circulate while students are working, offering help where needed. Make sure that they are putting the fir trees below the snowline and the alpine plants above it.

Biology • Topic 1 Plants 1.9

Graded activities

1 Students examine the plants that grown below the icy slopes – the pine trees and the fir trees. If you can, have some bark and fir needles on hand for students to handle. Note that fir trees have tough, thick bark to protect them from freezing, and needle shaped leaves with a thick waxy coating, to protect them from the cold. Make sure students record these salient facts in their writing.

2 Students look at the differences between plants growing in hot, dry conditions and those growing in cold, wet conditions. They should record the information in a table in their exercise books. You can take this in for marking to assess whether everyone has understood the concept of adaptation.

3 The students should apply all they have learned to a study of their own environment. They should examine their own environment and write a paragraph explaining the conditions (weather, climate) and ways in which local plants are suited to survive living in the area.

Consolidate and review

- Revise the different adaptations you've dealt with in the last few weeks. Have a quick quiz. Show a photo or picture of a plant and give the students 10 seconds to write down its name and where they think it grows.

- Ask: *How many different kinds of adapted leaves have we learned about?* Write a list of them on the board (needles, lettuce, spines etc.) Ask the same question about plant stems.

Differentiation

■ All of the students should be able to identify examples of how different plants are suited to cold and wet conditions.

● Many of the students will be able to compare plants in cold, wet conditions with plants in hot, dry areas.

▲ Some of the students will be able to do an analysis of the conditions where they live, and be able to say which plants are suited to live in these conditions.

Biology • Topic 1 Plants 1.10

1.10 Flowers and unusual plants

Student's Book pages 20–21

Biology learning objective
- Know that plants have roots, leaves, stems and flowers.

Resources
- Workbook pages 16 and 17

Classroom equipment
- a variety of fresh flowers – each student should have access to at least two different flowers
- a flower press or heavy books to press flowers between
- sheets of paper towel
- if possible, a small carnivorous plant such as a venus fly trap to show the students
- coloured pens or pencils

Scientific enquiry skills
- *Obtain and present evidence:* Observe and compare objects, living things and events; present results in drawings, bar charts and tables.
- *Consider evidence and approach:* Make generalisations and begin to identify simple patterns in results.

Key words
- **flower**
- **petal**
- **pollen**
- **nutrients**

> ⚠ Students should avoid all poisonous plants and should check with an adult before picking any flowers to ensure that they are not poisonous.

Scientific background

Flowers contain *pollen* and form the fruits and seeds in a plant.

The *petals* of a flower are often brightly coloured to attract insects. Flowers can also be highly scented. Petals come in many different varieties of shape, size and colour. Not all flowers have the same number of petals.

At this stage the students do not need to know about pollination; they will be learning about this in Stage 5 of this course. The students should be able to identify the petals of a flower and be able to compare the size, shape and colour of different flowers.

Most plants absorb *nutrients* from the soil, but some, for example pitcher plants and the venus fly trap, are adapted to do it in other ways.

Introduction

- Hold up one of the flowers you have brought to class. Ask students to say ways in which they think the flower attracts bees and other insects.
- Take the flower apart and count the petals.
- Carefully lay the petals down on some paper towel, so that students can come up and examine them.

Teaching and learning activities

- Turn to page 20 of the Student's Book. Ask students what the role of the flower is. They will probably answer that it is to attract insects. Praise this answer but add that the most important job is that the flower grows the seed and fruit of the plant. Say that they will learn more about this in Stage 5.
- Read through the text on Student's Book pages 20 and 21 and answer the questions as a class. Discuss any unusual plants or flowers that the students might be familiar with. If possible, bring in a small carnivorous plant to show the students (for example, a venus fly trap), let them examine it and suggest why it traps flies and insects.
- Show the class a large variety of fresh flowers. Ask: *How could you sort the flowers into groups?* Elicit that there are several ways the flowers could be sorted, for example by colour, size, number of petals, scent etc. Can any of the flowers be sorted into more than one group?

Biology • Topic 1 Plants 1.10

Graded activities

1 The students should draw and label their two flowers on page 16 of their Workbooks. Circulate and encourage the students to draw the flowers as accurately as they can. They should compare their two flowers by counting the number of petals, and by looking at the shape, size and colour of the petals.

2 In groups, the students should then use the flower press. They should carefully place their flowers between two sheets of paper and put this into the press. If you do not have a flower press, use a telephone directory, or any heavy book like a dictionary or encyclopaedia. You will need to leave the flowers to dry over at least a week.

In the meantime, the students should start preparing their posters. Once the flowers are dry, they should stick them to their poster and write a short description of each flower.

3 Give each group a selection of fresh flowers and again ask them to describe ways in which they are similar or different. Explain that the bright, colourful parts are petals. Get the students to choose three different flowers and let them carefully pull off the petals. They should count the petals and construct a bar chart on page 17 of their Workbook. Talk through the steps to construct the bar graph. The different flowers should go along the horizontal axis and the number of petals up the vertical axis.

Ask: *What do you notice about the size of the petals and the number of petals?* (Generally, the greater the number of petals there are, the smaller the petals will be.)

Consolidate and review

- Revise the different parts of a plant and ask what the function of each part is. Students should be able to identify the leaves, stem, roots, flowers and petals.

- Have a quick class quiz. Make up ten questions and read them out. The students write the answers in their exercise books. This will give you a good indication of who has grasped the new terms and concepts and who still needs help.

Differentiation

■ All of the students should be able to accurately draw and label their flowers. They will be able to count the petals and make a basic scientific comparison between the two flowers.

● Most of the students should be able to press their flowers and undertake the research for their poster with little or no help. Less able students may need some help writing the description of their flower.

▲ Some of the students should be able to count the petals of the flowers and construct a bar graph independently. Less able students will need additional help and guidance to draw their bar graphs.

Biology • Topic 1 Plants Consolidation

Consolidation

Student's Book page 22
Biology learning objectives
- Know that plants have roots, leaves, stems and flowers.
- Explain observations that plants need water and light to grow.
- Know that water is taken in through the roots and transported through the stem.
- Know that plants need healthy roots, leaves and stems to grow well.
- Know that plant growth is affected by temperature.

Resources
- Workbook page 18
- Assessment Sheets B1, B2 and B2

Classroom equipment
- coloured pens or pencils

Looking back
- Use the summary points to review the key knowledge areas students have learned in this topic.
- Ask students to make a plant poster on page 18 of their Workbooks.

How well do you remember?

You may use the revision and consolidation activities on page 22 either as a test or as a paired class activity. If you are using them as a class activity, you may prefer to let the students do the tasks orally. Circulate as they discuss the pictures and observe the students to see who is confident and who is unsure of the concepts.

Some suggested answers
1. It would die. Plants need water to grow and stay healthy.
2. Not all plant roots are the same. Tap roots grow deep into the soil and are swollen with water. Fibrous roots spread out widely to capture as much water as possible.
3. So that they grow well and survive in their environments.
4. Diversity is good. Different plants are suited to different types of habitats and environments.
5. Answers might include: a plant in a hot desert has a thick stem to store water and has deep roots. A plant on a cold mountain has shallow roots and does not grow very tall.

Assessment

A more formal assessment of the students' understanding of the topic can be undertaken using Assessment Sheets B1, B2 and B3. These can be completed in class or as a homework task.

Students following Cambridge Assessment International Education Primary Science Curriculum Framework will write progression tests set and supplied by Cambridge at this level and feedback will be given regarding their achievement levels.

Assessment Sheet answers

Sheet B1
1. Students' diagrams. [4]
2. true / true / false [3]
3.

Difference	Explanation	[2]
Water plants can have much weaker stems than land plants.	They don't have to support leaves and they can be flexible to give way in water currents.
Water plants can have much bigger leaves than land plants.	They can float in water and don't need strong stems to support them.

4. The more light a plant gets, the more food it can make through photosynthesis. Too much sunlight can damage plants, however. [1]

Sheet B2
1. water / sunlight / warmth / cold / temperature [5]
2. They provide food for animals. Desert plants can provide water for animals. [2]
3. false / true / false [3]

Sheet B3
1. tap roots / water / fibrous roots / stores [4]
2. true / true / false [3]
3. It has small, spiny leaves. It has a fat stem that holds lots of water. [2]
4. bee [1]

Student's Book answers

Pages 2–3
1. From rainwater.
2. Students trace from the roots, through the stem to the leaves and flowers.
3. Water and minerals from the soil, sunlight, and carbon dioxide from the air.

Pages 4–5
1. They anchor the plant in the soil. They absorb water and nutrients from the soil, which the plant needs to grow.
2. The first is a fibrous root, then a root that is storing food, then a tap root. The fibrous root is thin and spreads out wide to capture water; the tap root is long because it goes deep into the soil; the root that is storing food is much fatter than the other roots.
3. Desert plant – very long and deep, to get at water deep down. Weed – shallow and branching, to find water in cracks. Mountain plant - branching and deep, to hold tight onto rocky slopes, and find the soil between the rocks to grow in.

Pages 6–7
1. Students identify stem (or trunk), and leaves.
2. They are absorbed by the roots and then transported up the stem to the other parts of the plants.
3. Cabbage – shallow roots as there is no need for a big anchor. Tree – long tap root to anchor it deeply into the ground, so the wind doesn't blow it over.

Pages 8–9
1. Plants can make their own food.
2. They use sunlight, carbon dioxide from the air, and water and mineral salts from the soil.
3. If the Sun stopped shining, plants would not be able to make food. There would be no food. It would be dark and cold. People and animals would die.

Pages 10–11
1. Steps 1–3 are the same.
2. Bean A is put in a warm place and Bean B is put in a cold place.
3. It will not grow.
4. Bean A will grow best because it has light, water and warmth.

Pages 12–13
1. The plant would struggle to grow and might die.
2. The plants with fertiliser had more nutrients to feed them, so they are healthier and bigger than the ones without fertiliser.
3. No, some soils have enough nutrients in them. Sandy soils often need more fertiliser than other soils.
4. 'Watered mechanically, or by people' – in other words watered on purpose and not by accident, such as through rain.
5. Irrigation makes the land wet, so you can grow plants there.
6. Animals that like to live in the dry desert now have to find somewhere else to live – so it disturbs the balance of nature. Also, irrigation is very expensive, so you have to be very rich to do this.

Pages 14–15
1. Any two from: roots, stem, leaves, flowers.
2. Like land plants, water plants have leaves, roots, stems and flowers, and they need sunlight to make food. Unlike land plants, water plants are suited to growing wholly or partially under the water.
3. Pondweed stems and leaves are supported by the water. When they are out of water they are too thin and weak to stand upright.

Pages 16–17
1. It doesn't rain often in the desert, and when it does, it only rains a little. So the cactus needs to store water.
2. In its folded stem. It opens up its folds to collect more water, then stores it in a swollen stem.
3. They need to reach very deep underground to find water.
4. To deter animals in the desert from eating the swollen stems, which are full of water.

Pages 18–19
1. Cold and with strong winds.
2. There will be very little soil and it will not be very rich in nutrients. The soil will be found in rocky clefts and gullies.
3. It is low-growing, with strong roots to grip the little soil it can find. Leaves are hard and waxy to deal with the cold.
4. The trees will grow poorly if the water in their leaves freezes.
5. It is too rocky and cold. Some areas are covered in snow.

Pages 20–21
1. Students' own answers. They should mention size, colour and shape.
2. Check that students can point to the petals of a flower.
3. Nutrients are natural substances in the soil or water which plants need for healthy growth. For example, minerals.
4. No. Some plants get their nutrients from dead insects and beetles.

Biology • Topic 2 Humans and animals

2.1 Life processes

Student's Book pages 24–25

Biology learning objective
- Know life processes common to humans and animals include nutrition (water and food), movement, growth and reproduction.

Resources
- Workbook pages 19 and 20
- DVD Activity B2: What animals like to eat

Classroom equipment
- pencils

Scientific enquiry skills
- *Ideas and evidence:* Collect evidence in a variety of contexts to answer questions or test ideas.
- *Obtain and present evidence:* Observe and compare objects, living things and events; present results in drawings, bar charts and tables.
- *Consider evidence and approach:* Draw conclusions from results and begin to use scientific knowledge to suggest explanations.

Key words
- life processes
- nutrition
- reproduce
- move
- sensitivity

⚠️ Make sure the playground activity is supervised. Warn students not to touch anything that they are not sure about. Students should be careful not to pick up anything poisonous. As this is an observation task, students can use pencils, rather than their fingers, to turn over leaves and insects.

Scientific background

There are seven *life processes* common to all living things:
- They can move (*movement*).
- They reproduce or have young living things like themselves (*reproduction*).
- They respond or react to stimuli (*sensitivity*).
- They grow (*growth*).
- They need food and water to stay alive (*nutrition*).
- They use oxygen from the air to help turn food into energy (*respiration*).
- They get rid of waste (*excretion*).

Animals can move by themselves but plants also move. They can move their leaves and flowers towards sunlight – a good example for students is a sunflower, which rotates towards the Sun.

Excretion and respiration are not covered at Stage 3. Reproduction in plants is covered in more detail in Stage 5.

Introduction

- Discuss living and non-living things. Students have learned about this in Stage 1 so they should understand that some things are alive and some things are not alive. Ask students: *How can you tell the difference between a living and a non-living thing?* Ask volunteers to come up in turn and write down one point each. Introduce the scientific term 'life processes'.

- Tell the class that scientists have special words that they use to describe the different life processes. Write the terms on the board and ask the students to tell you what they mean. Explain the word 'criteria' to students and show that we can use different criteria to decide if something is living or non-living.

Biology • Topic 2 Humans and animals 2.1

Teaching and learning activities

- Get the students to turn to pages 24 and 25 of their Student's Books. Students will already be familiar with the terms 'living' and 'non-living', but now get them to think about how we can identify these more formally. Students should examine the pictures and answer the questions. Ask students to compile a list of actions that living things do then link this to the text and the scientific terms for the life processes. Discuss any life processes that students are unsure about. Ensure that students know that this is a scientific discussion and they are discussing these terms scientifically – this should limit any disruption when discussing 'sensitive' terms, such as 'reproduction'.

- Try to get students to think about why these life processes are useful for living things. For example, movement is important for animals to hunt for food or find shelter. Plants can make their own food but need sunlight, so their movement is limited to moving towards light. Remind students of the shoebox maze investigation they did in Topic 1, where the plant grew (moved) towards the light.

Graded activities

1 Ask the students to choose an animal; they could draw a picture of it as well. They should write a paragraph about their animal saying how they know it is alive. For example, it can move, it eats food to grow and stay healthy, and it can have young.

2 In groups, the students should make a list of as many different ways animals move that they can think of. For example, flying, swimming, jumping, hopping, running, slithering. They should then make a poster and group animals according to the way they move. What do they notice about the groups? Can any of the animals be in more than one group? How did they decide which group to put them in? Display the posters and allow the groups to peer review them. They should offer both positive and negative feedback, and suggest ways the posters could be improved.

3 The students should work in pairs to collect evidence of the living things that they can find in the playground environment. They should fill in the relevant record sheets in their Workbooks on pages 19 and 20. One deals with animal life and one with plant life. Each pair should complete both sheets, although you may want to divide the workload, so that one student examines plant life and the other records, and then they swap roles.

Once you are back in the classroom, see how much common information was collected, especially about animals. You can draw up a class table or bar graph showing the results of your excursion. Draw up a tally chart and write the most common animals' names on the board then guide students in drawing a bar chart for the five most common animals.

Consolidate and review

- Talk about the criteria the students used to tell if something was a living thing or a non-living thing.
- Students can complete DVD Activity B2 about what different animals like to eat, as a fun activity to reinforce the idea that all animals need to eat.

Differentiation

■ All of the students should be able to write a paragraph about their chosen animal saying how they know it is alive with little or no help from the teacher.

● Most of the students will be able to group animals according the different ways that they move. All of the students should realise that some animals can move in more than just one way.

▲ Some of the students will be able to explain the life processes of an animal that they know, without referring to the list of life processes. They will be able to construct bar graphs with little or no help.

Biology • Topic 2 Humans and animals 2.2

2.2 Living and non-living things

Student's Book pages 26–27

Biology learning objective
- Describe differences between living and non-living things using knowledge of life processes.

Resources
- Workbook pages 21 and 22
- Video B4: Living and non-living things

Classroom equipment
- a pot plant
- pictures of an animal
- coloured pens or pencils

Scientific enquiry skills
- *Ideas and evidence:* Collect evidence in a variety of contexts to answer questions or test ideas.
- *Consider evidence and approach:* Make generalisations and begin to identify simple patterns in results.

⚠️ Make sure the playground activity is supervised. Warn students not to touch anything that they are not sure about.

Scientific background

Our world is made up of living and non-living things, which are interdependent. Plants, animals and people need non-living things like soil, water and air for survival. Some of these things share what seems to be a life process with living things – air moves, for example, – but it is not a living thing because it does not do all of the life processes. For example, it does not eat, excrete, reproduce etc.

Life processes are common to all living things. This unit attempts to get students to use the life processes that they have learned about to define what makes something living or non-living. In this way they are applying new methods of scientific observation and scientific terminology (reproduce, move, nutrition, sensitivity and growth) to their understanding of living and non-living things.

Introduction

- Ask the class: *Are you alive? How do you know?* Students might volunteer that they are breathing or moving. As they give answers, write down their responses on the board. Ask: *What other things do all living things do?* They should be able to name the life processes from the previous lesson. Add these to the list on the board.

- Point to the picture of an animal, or to the classroom pet. Ask: *What about this animal, is it alive?* Make a separate list on the board for the animal, alongside your list for humans. If no one has mentioned reproduction, sensitivity etc. ask more direct questions, for example, ask students: *Can this animal have babies? Is that one of the things living things can do? Shall I write it in the column for humans as well as animals?*

- Now show them your plant. Ask: *Is this a living thing?* Make a new column on the board, headed: Plants. See how many of the life processes the class can add.

Biology • Topic **2** Humans and animals 2.2

Teaching and learning activities

- Turn to pages 26 and 27 of the Student's Book. Discuss the differences between living and non-living things. Let the students work in pairs to look at the pictures and decide what is living and what is non-living. Circulate as they discuss the questions, offering help where necessary.
- Show the students Video B4 of living and non-living things. (This video is repeated here from Stage 1 in order for students to revise what they have learned about living and non-living things and for the teacher to address any misconceptions that less-able students may still have.) Take questions and have a whole-class discussion after the video. Can the class draw up a list of questions that you can use to find out if something is alive or not?
- Take the students outside to the school grounds. They should have their Workbooks with them and a pencil. They are going to look for living and non-living things carrying out the life processes.

Graded activities

Differentiation for these activities is through outcome. For example in activity 1 some students will be more confident when identifying things as living or non-living whereas others will need more prompting and reminding of the criteria. Similarly, in activity 2 and activity 3 more able students will provide a greater range of questions and a more detailed explanation referencing all seven life processes.

1 Students should look for living and non-living things in the school grounds and fill in the table in their Workbook on page 21. There is a column for 'I'm not sure' too. Once you are all back in the classroom, ask students if they have anything in the 'I'm not sure' column. Discuss each instance and help the students to reallocate the things they are unsure of.

2 Students then turn to page 22 of the Workbook and work individually to record the list of questions they used to work out if something is living. Let students work individually on this, so you can assess who has grasped the new terms and concepts. They should also draw three living and three non-living things.

3 In the last five minutes of the lesson, students attempt to answer the trick question: *Is fire alive?* Each student writes his or her name on a piece of paper along with the answer to the question. They will hand this in to you as they leave the class. Tell them to go through the lists on the board if they need help.

Consolidate and review

- The outing in the school grounds is a perfect opportunity for informal assessment. Circulate among the pairs, asking questions and noting who has grasped the concepts and who needs more help.
- Use other objects in the classroom to ask the question: *How do you know that this is non-living?* This will give you the negative list: it doesn't move, it doesn't breathe, etc.
- Get students to work in pairs and to discuss why they are living things and why other objects in their classroom are non-living things. They should be encouraged to use the scientific terms for the life processes that they have learned.

Differentiation

■ All of the students should be able to distinguish between living and non-living things.

● Most of the students should be able to answer the questions in the Workbook with little or no help. They should be able to draw three living and three non-living things and identify if any of the non-living things were once living.

▲ Some of the students will be able to name the life processes and will be able to explain that a fire is not living. The flames appear to move but it is not alive.

Big Cat

Students who have read *Big Cat The oak tree* may relate the learning in this lesson to the many different types of organisms, including plants and animals, described in this book. It provides a lively introduction to the topic of living things.

Biology • Topic 2 Humans and animals 2.3

2.3 Food for energy

Student's Book pages 28–29

Biology learning objective
- Explore and research exercise and the adequate, varied diet needed to keep healthy.

Resources
- Workbook pages 23 and 24
- Slideshow B3: Different foods
- Slideshow B4: Where do animals get their food?
- PCM B5: Food groups

Classroom equipment
- examples of foods from the different food groups (tin of sardines, piece of bread, piece of fruit, etc.)
- photographs of different meals, cut from newspapers and magazines
- coloured pens or pencils
- scissors

Scientific enquiry skills
- *Obtain and present evidence:* Present results in drawings, bar charts and tables.

Key words
- protein
- carbohydrates
- sugars
- fats
- vitamins

⚠️ Be sensitive to students' different economic and cultural backgrounds during the next few units. Supervise the students when they use scissors.

Scientific background

Food gives your body the energy and the materials that your body needs to grow, stay healthy, and repair injuries. The human body uses energy even at rest. Energy is needed to power the heart and lungs, as well as to move and think.

Foods are mixtures of different nutrients: *proteins, carbohydrates, sugars, fats, vitamins* and minerals.

Proteins are found in meat, fish, cheese and eggs as well as in pulses. Your body is built of proteins and it needs protein foods to help it to develop and repair itself.

Carbohydrates supply energy and are found in starchy foods like potatoes, pasta and rice as well as in sugars.

Fats are only needed in small quantities and are found in butter, dairy products, nuts and oils from plants. Fats also provide energy, and excess fat is stored under the skin.

Minerals and vitamins are found in small quantities in most foods, but are more concentrated in fruits and vegetables. You need vitamins and minerals to build healthy bones and teeth, and to prevent illness.

Introduction

- You will need to organise this activity carefully and perhaps tell classes being taught nearby that the start of your lesson might be noisier. Clear a space in the classroom and ask students to get up from their desks and stand in the space. Now ask them to follow your instructions. Say: *Run on the spot. Stop. Do ten jumping jacks. Stop. Run on the spot again. Stop. Do ten jumping jacks. Stop.* Then ask students to sit back at their desks.

- Ask: *How do you feel?* Students may say that they are out of breath, or that their hearts are beating faster. Ask them where they got the energy to do this activity. Some will say they were ordered to do it; some will say their bodies gave them the energy.

- Bring them to understand that their bodies gave them the energy to perform the actions but that the real energy came from the fuel they put into their bodies. Just as a car needs fuel and water to go, they need fuel and water too.

- Ask for volunteers to tell what they had for breakfast that morning. Write down the food items on the board. Be sensitive here, as different groups of people eat different kinds of meals. Also be very careful if you are teaching in a poorer region – there will be some students in your class who won't have

28

Biology • Topic 2 Humans and animals 2.3

had breakfast. If this is the case, and your budget allows, bring a piece of fruit or a piece of bread for each student and adapt the lesson slightly, saying you are giving them fuel. Emphasise that food is the fuel the body needs to live and grow.

Teaching and learning activities

- Demonstrate the foods that you have brought to class. Hold up the tin of sardines, for example, and ask: *What are these? Does anyone know what food group they belong to?* Explain what protein foods are and what they do for your body and write the heading 'protein' on the board. Underneath it, write 'fish'.

- Write the other food groups up on the board – fats, carbohydrates, sugars, vitamins and minerals – and explain each one using the text and pictures on pages 28 and 29 in the Student's Book. Ask students to tell you foods that they know, and add them to the board under the correct heading. Hold up each item of food you have brought to class and ask the students what it is. Then ask them what the food does. Write the food examples on the board under the correct heading.

- Now ask for random examples of food, and then ask volunteers to come up and write the food in the correct column. Gradually build up a board that contains a range of examples of foods from all five food groups.

- Explain to the students that most foods contain a mix of the food groups – so nuts, for example, contain proteins and fats, but we put them in the protein group because that's what they contain more of. Olive oil contains fats and vitamins, but it goes in the fats group, because that is what it contains more of. Show the students Slideshow B3 of a variety of different foods.

- Now get the students to turn to pages 28 and 29 of the Students Book. Ask them to look at the pictures and descriptions, and answer the questions in their groups. Circulate while they work, offering help where needed.

Graded activities

1 Ask the students to turn to the activity on page 23 of their Workbook. They should colour all the different food groups different colours, as instructed. Check this work in class, to make sure everyone is following the new terms and concepts.

2 Hand out pictures of different meals, cut from magazines. Encourage students to discuss the pictures. Ask: *Does your picture show a balanced meal? Does it have something from every food group in it?* Either ask each group to draw what they think a good meal would be or have a class discussion and ask students to debate why their meal is the best one.

3 Write a list of foods up on the board. These should be foods that students will be familiar with and might have at home. Ask students to examine the list of foods and record each food on the correct shelf on page 24 of the Workbook.

Consolidate and review

- Use PCM B5 to check whether the students have understood the new terms and concepts introduced in this unit. You will need one copy for each group. Cut along the dotted lines, as indicated, and shuffle the cut-up pieces well. The groups need to match each food group with examples of that food group and with the benefits of those foods to our bodies.

- Show the students Slideshow B4 to see if they can say where different animals get their food.

Differentiation

■ All of the students should understand that food gives you energy, that foods are of different types or groups and that each group gives something different to the body. They should be able to do the Workbook activity with little or no help.

● Most of the students should be able to say the names of the different food groups and give examples of some foods from each group. They should select the 'best' meal based on how healthy the meal is.

▲ Some of the students should be able to make a list of foods independently. They will be able to draw them in the correct place in their Workbook without any additional help.

Biology • Topic 2 Humans and animals 2.4

2.4 Eating the right food

Student's Book pages 30–31

Biology learning objective
- Explore and research exercise and the adequate, varied diet needed to keep healthy.

Resources
- Workbook pages 25 and 26
- DVD Activity B3: Food pyramid

Classroom equipment
- old newspapers and magazines
- glue
- scissors
- coloured pens or pencils

Scientific enquiry skills
- *Ideas and evidence:* Collect evidence in a variety of contexts to answer questions or test ideas.
- *Obtain and present evidence:* Observe and compare objects, living things and events; present results in drawings, bar charts and tables.

Key words
- **healthy**
- **fibre**
- **balanced**
- **diet**
- **food pyramid**

⚠ Supervise the students when they use scissors.

Scientific background

Your *diet* is the type of food you eat every day. A *healthy* diet is one that gives you all the right nutrients in the right amounts. Your diet needs to be *balanced*; that is, it should include all the main food groups in the correct quantities. To get a good balance of nutrients, you need to eat fruit and vegetables, cereals, and enough protein and carbohydrates to provide energy and building material for your body. Current scientific thinking puts the proportions at one serving of protein, one serving of carbohydrates and two servings of vegetables or fruits in a meal. It is also important to eat sufficient *fibre*, and to hydrate your body by taking in enough water. You need between five and eight glasses of water a day, depending on your body size.

The proportions of foods from the different groups in a healthy, balanced diet can be represented as a *food pyramid*.

Introduction

- Discuss the 'cupboard' activity from the previous lesson. Were there lots of protein foods? Were there lots of carbohydrate foods? Talk about the fact that many carbohydrate foods, such as cereals, pasta and flour, can be dried for storage so many people keep them at home. Meat and fish need to be eaten fresh, so there would be less of these, although there may be some tins of fish in the cupboard. Fruit and vegetables are often bought on the day that they will be cooked, so that they don't go rotten. However some vegetables, like potatoes, onions and pumpkins, can be stored for a long time. Fats like olive oil can also be stored for a long time in a dark bottle.

- Discuss what the students think a 'balanced meal' is. Do they think it means having exactly the same quantity of meat, vegetables, carbohydrates and fats? Or does it mean having a balanced quantity of these foodstuffs, according to what our body needs? (The latter, of course.)

Teaching and learning activities

- Get the students to draw what they consider to be a balanced meal in their exercise books. They can talk about the activity in pairs, and then they should work individually to draw what they consider a balanced meal on the plate. Circulate while they are discussing and drawing, offering help where needed. Students should end up with a plate that is roughly divided into four – one for protein, one for carbohydrates and two for vegetables. Take feedback and allow variation – some students may have a fruit instead of a vegetable, or a plate of stew. Get them to label each foodstuff. Remind students to draw a glass of water next to the plate, if they have forgotten to show any liquid.

- Turn to page 30 of the Student's Book and ask students to look at the girl's meal. Ask them to compare the girl's meal to the one which they drew. Get them to name each part of the meal.

Biology • Topic **2** Humans and animals 2.4

Ask: *Where is the protein? Where are the carbohydrates? Does this person have any fruit or vegetables for their meal? Do you think this is a balanced meal?*

- Students should now study the food pyramid on page 31. You can draw a basic pyramid on the board and then ask students to come up and add different foods to it. Explain that the pyramid shows how much of each food group we need – more carbohydrates (at the bottom) and a very little fat or sugar (at the top).
- You can get students to make their own food pyramids in their groups, using pictures from old newspapers and magazines.

Graded activities

1 In pairs, students should discuss what they have learned about food pyramids and balanced diets so far. They should take turns to explain a food pyramid to their partner. Circulate while they are doing this so you can assess how well they have grasped the concepts.

2 Students should make a list of the foods they ate yesterday and record their information in the food pyramid in their Workbooks on page 25. They should also write down what they should eat more of and what they should eat less of. Take this work in for assessment to make sure that everyone has grasped the new terms and concepts.

3 The students should extend their knowledge by writing a healthy menu for a Stage 3 class for a day. They should do this on page 26 of their Workbooks. Allow some leeway here, but when assessing the work, make sure that there is a balance of good food across the day, as well as enough hydration (at least five glasses of water).

Consolidate and review

- Tell the students what you had for breakfast. Ask them if you had a balanced meal. Ask: *How can you help me? What should I change?*
- Let the students complete DVD Activity B3 to reinforce what they have learned in this unit.
- Have a quick five-question quiz. Instruct: *Write down the name of a protein food. Write down the name of a carbohydrate food.* etc. Mark the test in class.

Differentiation

■ All of the students should be able to understand that there are different food groups, and be able to mention at least one example from each food group. They should be able to advise their partner about what to eat less/more of.

● Most of the students should be able to identify three or more foods from each group and understand that we need to eat more of some of them than of others. They should be able to draw their food pyramid and say if their food intake for the day was healthy or unhealthy. They should suggest ways they can improve their diet.

▲ Some of the students should be able to explain why you need to eat a balanced meal, and explain in which proportions the food groups should be consumed. They will be able to create a balanced and healthy menu for their class with little or no help.

Biology • Topic 2 Humans and animals 2.5

2.5 Eating the wrong food

Student's Book pages 32–33

Biology learning objective
- Know that some foods can be damaging to health, e.g. very sweet and fatty foods.

Resources
- Workbook pages 27 and 28

Classroom equipment
- packaging from chips, sweets and other junk food
- old newspapers and magazines
- scissors and glue

Scientific enquiry skills
- *Plan investigative work:* Suggest ideas, make predictions and communicate these.
- *Obtain and present evidence:* Observe and compare objects, living things and events; present results in drawings, bar charts and tables.

Key words
- unhealthy
- junk food

⚠ Supervise the students when they use scissors.

Scientific background

An unbalanced diet contains too many processed foods like chips, sweets and salty or fatty snacks, and can be *unhealthy*. This kind of food is commonly called *junk food*, because it is low in nutrient-value and high in potentially damaging fats and sugars. A diet which features a lot of junk food is not a healthy diet, as the proportion of sugars, fats and salt is too high, and there are not enough proteins and vitamins and minerals. A diet which includes too many sugars can lead to weight gain and diseases such as diabetes. A diet with too much fat consumption can lead to heart disease and weight gain.

Introduction

- Bring a selection of junk food packaging into class or ask students to bring some in, then display it on your table. Ask: *Which of these foods do you like to eat? Which are you allowed to eat? Why are you not allowed to eat these foods?* Elicit the response that they taste delicious but are bad for us.
- Talk about the way that sweets give you a short burst of energy, but that eating too many of them can rot your teeth. Explain that chips and fatty foods can also give you energy, but that the energy which your body doesn't need is stored in fatty tissue which can increase your weight. Say that the long-term effect of too much of this kind of food in your diet is that fats can build up around your heart and can cause a heart attack when you are older.
- In groups, let students examine one of the items of junk food. They should read the package and find out what ingredients go into making the food. You can list some of these on the board. Ask: *How many of these ingredients are natural? How many are made chemicals? What effect do you think they have on your body?*

Teaching and learning activities

- Look at the pictures on pages 32 and 33 of the Student's Book. Ask the students to study the images and answer the questions in their groups. Circulate while they are working, offering help where it is needed. Ask: *Who eats this kind of food every day? Who eats this kind of food once a week? Who eats this kind of food on special occasions?* Unless you feel it is better to exclude this food entirely, explain that most junk food is fine if it is eaten only occasionally, such as on special occasions, but that eating it regularly is unhealthy. Modify your response depending on your classroom context.
- Explain to the students that our bodies need the vitamins and minerals we get from fruit and vegetables, protein to help grow strong nails and hair and carbohydrates for energy. Without a good balance of these food groups, we can get diseases or weaken our bodies.

Biology • Topic 2 Humans and animals 2.5

- Talk about the way the food in the picture has been prepared. Ask: *How are the chips made? How was the burger made?* Discuss whether there are alternative ways of preparing these foods that are healthier. (For example, baked potatoes, grilled meat etc.)

Graded activities

1 In pairs, the students should cut out some pictures of food (or draw some food items) and make a food pyramid poster that can be displayed in the school's lunch hall or canteen as part of a healthy eating campaign. They should use the knowledge they have gained in this topic to help them to create their poster.

2 Students should write a junk food log based on the junk food they have eaten during the last week. They fill in the table in their Workbooks on page 27. In one column they should write all the junk food they can remember and in the other column they should write down healthy alternatives. Try not to be judgmental about students' food choices – they are just learning about healthy foods and may not have much choice about the foods they eat at home. However, you may want to suggest some small changes to diet to the class as a whole if it seems appropriate.

3 Students should prepare a balanced menu for a day by cutting out pictures from old newspapers and magazines and sticking them onto page 28 of their Workbooks in the correct proportions – one quarter protein, two quarters vegetables and fruit, and one quarter carbohydrates.

Consolidate and review

- Quickly revise what benefits the various food groups provide. Ask: *What do protein foods do for you? What food group gives you energy? What goodness does a potato have?* (Carbohydrates, and vitamins and minerals.) Then ask: *What could you do that would make a potato into a bad food choice?* (Deep fry it and cover it with salt.)
- Talk about what alternatives there are for sweets. Talk about pieces of fruit, which not only taste sweet but also give you vitamins and minerals.
- Get one of the students to sum up the 'key message' of the lesson in one sentence.

Differentiation

■ All of the students should be able to create a balanced food pyramid poster with little or no help. More able students may add slogans and other information to their posters as part of their healthy eating campaign.

● Most of the students should understand that junk food (food that is very sweet, or very fatty) can damage your health and that this is why it should be avoided.

▲ Some of the students should be able to create a balanced menu based on one quarter protein, two quarters vegetables and fruit, and one quarter carbohydrates with little or no help. Less able students may need help understanding quarters and halves.

Biology • Topic 2 Humans and animals 2.6

2.6 Exercise

Student's Book pages 34–35

Biology learning objective
- Explore and research exercise and the adequate, varied diet needed to keep healthy.

Resources
- Workbook pages 29 and 30

Classroom equipment
- mats or towels on which to do exercises
- coloured pens or pencils

Scientific enquiry skills
- *Ideas and evidence:* Collect evidence in a variety of contexts to answer questions or test ideas.
- *Plan investigative work:* Suggest ideas, make predictions and communicate these.
- *Obtain and present evidence:* Measure using simple equipment and record observations in a variety of ways.
- *Consider evidence and approach:* Draw conclusions from results and begin to use scientific knowledge to suggest explanations.

Key words
- exercise
- flexible
- stamina

⚠️ Make sure that students are wearing suitable clothing for doing exercise – they should be in gym clothes or loose clothes in which they can move freely. Ensure that students do not over-strain themselves in this lesson as it is meant to be instructive and fun. Be sensitive to modesty issues, which may be cultural or religious.

Scientific background

Exercise builds strong bones and muscles and keeps your heart, which is the muscle that pumps blood around the body, healthy. The human body is best suited to move – to run and catch food, to bend and gather food, to work hard and then rest. It is not designed for sitting for long periods of time. Everyone needs to exercise his or her muscles and bones regularly to stay healthy.

You can build strength, *flexibility* and *stamina* through regular exercise. Weight-bearing exercise builds strength, stretching exercises build flexibility, and endurance work builds stamina.

Introduction

- The first part of this lesson needs to be conducted outdoors. It's best to do this unit on a day when the weather is good, so if the weather is unsuitable you can move on to Units 2.7 and 2.8 about senses and then return to this exercise unit later.
- Take the class outside to the school field or playground. Explain that this unit is all about exercise and the ways that it affects the body. Explain that you are going to do a series of exercises as a scientific experiment.

- Make sure everyone is comfortably dressed for the lesson and that you have mats or towels for the exercises as well as water for the students to drink. Say: *Are you ready? Then let's go!*

Teaching and learning activities

- In pairs students should look at the photographs of the activities and answer the questions on pages 34–35 of the Student's Book. Emphasise to the class that exercise means a person is using their body well, and letting it do what it is best suited to do.
- Ask students what they understand by the words 'strength', 'stamina' and 'flexibility'. Ask: *Why is it useful to be strong? Why is it useful to have stamina? Why is it useful to be flexible?* Ask students if they can think of any examples where strength, stamina or flexibility is important.

Biology • Topic 2 Humans and animals 2.6

Graded activities

As this is a practical investigation, it is recommended that the students work in mixed ability groups for this activity. Differentiation should be through the level of support the students receive as they work on the activity, as well as by outcome (please see guidance in the 'Differentiation' box right).

1 Before they exercise, ask the students how they are feeling, while their bodies are at rest. Get them to breathe in and out. They should notice that they are breathing gently and their heart beat is regular and slow. Show them that their skin is a normal colour and not flushed. Ask them to run on the spot for 60 seconds. Then ask: *What is different from one minute ago? In what way has your breathing changed?* Then get them to listen to, or feel, their heart beat. Ask: *In what way is your heart beat different from one minute ago? Look around you – is anyone flushed and sweating? What parts of their body have been working?* (They should mention heart and lungs, as well as the obvious legs, arms etc.).

2 As a whole class ask individuals to come up and demonstrate exercises that they know. Get the class to say whether the exercise being demonstrated builds strength, stamina or flexibility.

3 Explain to students that running is an endurance exercise – the more you run, the further you can go and the fitter you can get. Say: *Now we are going to do some strength-building exercises.*

Demonstrate sit-ups and push-ups yourself or by instructing a student. Then get the students to do a set of sit-ups and push-ups. Students should aim for ten repetitions of each, but if they are not able to do that many, they should just do as many as they can.

Groups should discuss the running and the exercises. They should talk about the way that they felt before the exercise, immediately after it, and now. Circulate and listen to the discussions. Make sure everyone is mentioning heart rate, breathing and skin changes. Ask groups: *If you did this three times a week, what do you think would happen, over time?*

Students should return to group work to design an exercise programme for a Stage 3 student. After the group discussion they should work individually to record their exercise programme on page 29 of their Workbooks.

Consolidate and review

- The students should follow their exercise programme for a month and record their results. Get a few students to show the class their programme. Take feedback on their progress at least once a week. Tell students they should write a paragraph at the end of each week about their programme as well as their results.

- Students should complete the activity in the Workbook on page 30. They draw a picture of themselves doing the exercise they like the most and then write about why they think that form of exercise is good for them.

Differentiation

■ All of the students should be able to say the way that they felt before and after exercise.

● Most of the students should be able to demonstrate or describe an exercise that improves stamina, strength or flexibility.

▲ Some of the students will be able to create an interesting and varied exercise programme. Circulate and check that the programmes are not over ambitious or too easy. All of the students should be able to keep a record of how well their exercise programme is going over the course of one month.

Biology • Topic 2 Humans and animals 2.7

2.7 Your senses

Student's Book pages 36–37

Biology learning objective
- Explore human senses and the ways we use them to learn about our world.

Resources
- Workbook pages 31, 32 and 33
- PCM B6: Testing your senses
- DVD Activity B4: My senses

Classroom equipment
- watch or clock with seconds hand
- blindfolds
- different foods to taste
- different objects to touch

Scientific enquiry skills
- *Ideas and evidence:* Collect evidence in a variety of contexts to answer questions or test ideas.
- *Plan investigative work:* With help, think about collecting evidence and planning fair tests.
- *Obtain and present evidence:* Measure using simple equipment and record observations in a variety of ways.

Key words
- brain
- interpret

⚠ Make sure that the foods being tasted are not harmful and that students do not have any allergies. Ensure that the items being touched are not dangerous. Avoid sharp edges or fragile objects.

Scientific background

All living things, including animals and human beings, need to know what is going on in the world around them. They need to know when danger is coming, where to find good food, and who the creatures around them are. To access this information, they use their senses.

Vision tells us where things are and what they look like. Hearing helps us to work out the position of something and enables us to communicate. Smell and taste are important because they help us to choose between safe and dangerous foods and substances. Touch lets us know what things feel like and when they are near.

The sense organs (eyes, ears, nose, mouth and skin) pass information through the nervous system to the *brain*, which *interprets* it and tells us the way to react in a given situation.

Introduction

- Have students look around them. Ask them what they can see. Tell them they have one minute to write down everything they can see. Time them. The student with the longest correct list wins. Now say: *Imagine if you could not see. Just think about how many things you would be missing.*

- Talk about the senses. Draw out students' prior knowledge. Ask questions like: *What do you hear with? How do you know someone is walking behind you? How do you find out if something is hot?* Students should know the answers to these questions from Stages 1 and 2.

- Start an open discussion about the senses. Ask: *Are senses important? What are senses for?* Write down students' ideas on the board, without correcting any wrong ideas. Tell the class you will all look at these ideas later, and see which ones are correct.

Teaching and learning activities

- Get the students to turn to pages 36 and 37 of the Student's Book. Look at the pictures and discuss the different senses. Ask: *How does hearing tell you the position of something?* Talk about noises that are close and noises that are far away. What can the students hear in the classroom? What can they hear outside?

- Ask: *Why is it important that you can taste whether things are bad?* Get the students to think about how this sense helps to keep them safe.

- Explain that the senses send messages to the brain, which interprets the messages and then tells you what to do. You can explain that the nerves in

Biology • Topic 2 Humans and animals 2.7

the sense organs send messages along a path of nerves in a split second, and the brain responds immediately. Ask: *How quickly do you pull your hand away if you touch something hot?* Explain that that is how fast your brain works, in sending a message to your skin telling you to move your hand away.

- Let the students work in their groups to look at the four pictures and identify what senses the children in the pictures are using, and what messages their brains are sending to the sense organs.
- Have a whole-class discussion about which senses students think are their strongest. Some may have a very good sense of taste, others of smell. Ask them to give you concrete examples of why they say one sense is stronger than the others.
- Students can complete DVD Activity B4 to recap what they have already learned about the senses in Stages 1 and 2.

Graded activities

1 Students work individually to write down all the sounds they can hear with their eyes closed. They record the sounds in their Workbooks on page 31.

2 Working in pairs, students use PCM B6 to design a taste experiment. Ask students to make sure their test is fair. What will they keep the same? What will they change? Have each pair test at least five different tastes. Some ideas could be: a piece of fruit, some bread, cheese, processed meat – anything easily on hand, like the items in their lunchboxes. Get the students to record the results of their fair tests in the table on page 32 of their Workbook.

Still working in pairs, students use PCM B6 again, to design a touch experiment. What will they keep the same this time? What will they change? Have each pair test at least five different touches. Some ideas could be: half a grape, some butter, cotton wool, pencil shavings, an eraser – again, anything that is readily available. Get the students to record the results of their fair tests in the table on page 33 of their Workbook.

3 The students should try and communicate to other members of their group without speaking. How easy is it for the group to understand what the student is 'saying' without being able to hear them? Get the students to communicate feelings such as: I am afraid, I am hungry, I am angry.

Ask: *Was it easy or difficult to understand? How important is it to be able to communicate using all of your senses?* Ask the students to write a paragraph where they imagine they have lost one of their senses: they could describe being at a sports stadium, buying food in a cafe, crossing the road, etc. What senses do they need? What if one or more of their senses was not working?

Consolidate and review

- Give students different scenarios and ask them which senses they would use to tell what is going on around them. For example: It starts to rain; you discover the milk in the fridge has gone sour; when you are standing outside you know your favourite TV programme has started and your mother is cooking your favourite meal.
- Have a quick test. Ask students to work in pairs to write down the names of the senses. When they have both written the senses they should swap pages with their partner and their partner writes down what each sense does.
- Ask the students to look at the list you made on the board at the beginning of the lesson. Talk about each idea and tick the ones that are correct. Change or rub out the ideas that are incorrect or misguided.

Differentiation

■ All of the students should be able to record the sounds that they heard in their Workbooks with little or no help.

● Most of the students should be able to plan a fair test with some help. They will be able to complete PCM B6 and undertake the test with little or no help.

▲ Some of the students should be able to imagine what life would be like if one of their senses were not working. They may relate this to people who are deaf or blind.

37

Biology • Topic 2 Humans and animals 2.8

2.8 How your senses help you

Student's Book pages 38–39

Biology learning objective
- Explore human senses and the ways we use them to learn about our world.

Resources
- Workbook pages 34 and 35
- Slideshow B5: Braille
- Visit to an institution for the sight-impaired, or visit of a sight-impaired person to the class

Classroom equipment
- blindfolds

Scientific enquiry skills
- *Plan investigative work:* Suggest ideas, make predictions and communicate these.
- *Obtain and present evidence:* Observe and compare objects, living things and events.

Key words
- blind
- braille

⚠️ Help the students to blindfold each other for the activities and make sure the classroom is clear of objects and that the students take the activity seriously.

Scientific background

Your senses give you information about the world around you and protect you from danger. People who lack one of the sense organs have to adapt to a world that can feel unsafe to them. *Blind* (sight-impaired) people use their organs of touch (hands/skin) to read the imprint of words on a page in a special system called *braille*. People who cannot hear learn to read sign language, which is a language that uses the hands and face to transmit meaning.

Introduction

- Try to arrange for the class to visit an institution for the sight-impaired. The Society for the Blind in some countries allows visits, and in many places they will also send a person to speak to your class. If this can be arranged, then re-order the lesson around that. While the visit is in progress, tell students they should behave and stay together in a cohesive group.
- Discuss what the world would be like if you couldn't see. Encourage the students to give you ideas and get them to ask questions about how a person would do everyday activities, like eat, or read, or walking to the shops.

- Hand out a blindfold to each student and ask them to turn to page 34 of the Workbook. Tell them to put on their blindfold and try to draw a picture of their family in the space provided. They can use their hands to guide them on the page, but they must not cheat.
- Let them compare their drawing with their partner's. What is similar? What is different? How difficult or easy did they find the activity?

Teaching and learning activities

- In their pairs, encourage the students to read pages 38 and 39 of the Student's Book. They should talk about the pictures of the sight-impaired people and discuss the questions.
- Show the students Slideshow B5, which has some pictures of braille.
- Talk about the 'super senses' some animals have. Ask: *Do you know any other animals that have 'super senses'?* Allow students the freedom to imagine different scenarios. For example, if they had to choose a 'super sense', what would it be? Why? Get individuals to explain their choices.

Biology • Topic 2 Humans and animals 2.8

Graded activities

1 Ask students to imagine they are blindfolded. They should then think about what they do on a normal day and write down everything they would find difficult. What could they do to make things easier?

2 Visit the Society for the Blind, or invite a sight-impaired person to come and speak to the class about what their life is like. Arrange in advance for one student to welcome the visitor and another to thank him or her.

3 Tell the students to imagine that one strange day they woke up and they couldn't taste or smell anything! Ask for ideas about ways in which the day would be very different from their normal day. Get volunteers to give ideas, and write them down on the board. For example: you couldn't smell when breakfast was ready, or taste the food. What about brushing your teeth – what would that feel like? When you were eating, would you know when you were full? What about if someone gave you something awful to eat? Would you know? Would you eat it? After the class discussion, the students should write a short story about this in their Workbooks on page 35.

Consolidate and review

- Share the drawing of your family that you did while blindfolded and explain the difficulties you had. Encourage other pairs in the class to share their findings too.
- Have a whole-class discussion, either after your visit to the Society or after your visitor has left. What new information did the students learn? Make a table on the board to record the information. In the left column write things like how you eat, how you read, how you walk to the shops. In the right column include information you elicit from the class.

Differentiation

■ All of the students should understand that people who lack one sense, like sight or hearing, live lives that are challenging.

● Most of the students should know what kinds of adaptations people who lack a sense need to make in order to function in the world, for example, ways in which blind people adapt to living in a world designed for the sighted.

▲ Some of the students should be able to contrast and compare their life with that of a person who lacks a sense, for example like sight or hearing.

Biology • Topic 2 Humans and animals 2.9

2.9 Classifying living things (1)

Student's Book pages 40–41

Biology learning objective
- Sort living things into groups, using simple features and describe rationale for groupings.

Resources
- Workbook pages 36 and 37

Classroom equipment
- photocopies of pages 40 and 41 of the Student's Book: one set per group
- scissors and glue
- large sheets of paper
- coloured pens or pencils

Scientific enquiry skills
- *Obtain and present evidence:* Observe and compare objects, living things and events.
- *Consider evidence and approach:* Make generalisations and begin to identify simple patterns in results.

Key words
- classify
- mammal
- reptile
- insect
- antennae

⚠️ Supervise the students when they use scissors.

Scientific background

Scientists *classify* living things into groups, according to common features. The first big division is plants and animals. Animals are then further divided into vertebrates (animals with backbones) and invertebrates (animals without backbones). Vertebrates are further divided into fish, *reptiles*, *mammals*, amphibians and birds. Invertebrates include worms, arachnids, myriapods, crustaceans, *insects* and molluscs.

At this level the distinction between vertebrates and invertebrates is not made. This unit focuses on the common features of mammals, reptiles and insects, and the scientific process of classification. For example, one common feature of the insects is their *antennae*. The remaining animal groups are addressed in Unit 2.10.

Introduction

- Ask the students what they know about living things. (They should mention the seven life processes.) Ask them if this means that all animals are the same. (They should say no, we can see that animals are different.) Encourage them to point out ways that animals are different – different limbs, different skin and fur, different habitats, for example.

- Explain that we can group animals according to these differences and similarities. Explain that humans are mammals. Ask the students what features humans have that might allow us to identify other mammals. Introduce the idea that mammals give birth to live young, if this has not come out already in the answer students have given you. Ask: *How many mammals can you name?* (Answers will include humans, dogs, cats, cows, horses etc.) Ask: *What other features do mammals all have in common?* (They have the seven life processes, but they also all feed on their mother's milk when they are young.) Make sure students get these two salient points about mammals. You can write them on the board, under the heading 'mammals'.

- You can point out that a snake is a reptile and repeat the above exercise for reptiles. (They have dry scales that cover their bodies and they are cold blooded).

- Insects have six legs, and a hard outer covering. Some insects have wings.

- Write the names of the different groups of animals on the board, and add their common features as the discussion continues.

Biology • Topic 2 Humans and animals 2.9

Teaching and learning activities

- Ask the students to turn to pages 40 and 41 of their Student's Books. Encourage them to look at all the photographs of animals on the pages. Ask the students to name each animal.
- Once you are sure that the students can identify each animal, get them to work in their groups to answer the questions. They can use the notes you wrote on the board to help them. Circulate and answer questions where necessary.
- The students then complete the activity on page 36 of their Workbooks. The diagram shows groups of animals. They need to list as many animals as they can in each bubble. While they are doing this, circulate and correct as necessary.
- Keep the animal group names on the board for the next unit.

Graded activities

1 Give each group a photocopy of pages 40 and 41 of the Student's Book. They should cut out the pictures of the animals, and then sort them into groups with common features. Then they give each group a name. The groups can make a poster of their animal collection by sticking the animals in their groups on a large sheet of paper. Make sure each group has a name, for example mammals, reptiles etc.

Now get the students to write underneath each set of animals, what criteria they used to decide that the animals all belonged together in a group. If this activity is becoming unwieldy, sub-divide the student groups, and give each smaller group one section to deal with.

2 Students complete the activity on page 37 of their Workbook. They draw and describe their favourite animal, and say which group it belongs to.

3 Ask students to do some research to find out about an insect that lives in your local environment. Is the insect considered a pest? Are there measures to control it? What harm does it do? They can then draw and label a picture of the insect.

Consolidate and review

- Have a class guessing game. Write the names of certain animals on pieces of paper. Give each student a piece of paper. The student comes to the front of the class and acts out the animal, while the rest of the students have to guess what he/she is. Once they have guessed the animal's name, they must say what group it belongs to.
- If you are able to get hold of videos about animals or have access to the internet, then show one to the class. There are many documentaries available about animals and animal lives.

Differentiation

■ All of the students should be able to sort most of the animals into groups with shared features, and explain what those shared features are. Most of the students will be able to give a name to the groups (mammals, reptiles, insects) they create, and say what features of each animal make it a member of that group.

● Some of the students will be able to write down a list of the criteria used to test the inclusion of an animal in a specific group.

▲ Some of the students will be able to independently research a insect that lives in their local environment. They will be able to draw an accurate picture of it and say if it is a pest and what measures are taken to control it.

Biology • Topic 2 Humans and animals 2.10

2.10 Classifying living things (2)

Student's Book pages 42–43

Biology learning objective
- Sort living things into groups, using simple features and describe rationale for groupings.

Resources
- Workbook pages 38 and 39
- PCM B7: Animal groups
- Slideshow B6: Animal groups
- Slideshow B7: More animal groups

Classroom equipment
- coloured pens or pencils

Scientific enquiry skills
- *Obtain and present evidence:* Observe and compare objects, living things and events.
- *Consider evidence and approach:* Draw conclusions from results and begin to use scientific knowledge to suggest explanations.

Key words
- **fish**
- **bird**
- **amphibian**

Scientific background

This unit introduces further animal groups to the students. *Fish* have fins instead of legs, are covered in scales and live in water. *Birds* have two legs, feathers, a beak and wings. They are warm blooded and lay eggs. *Amphibians* have gills, like fish, but can also breathe air, often through their skins. They lay their eggs in water. Some animals, such as dolphins and whales, might appear to be fish because they live in water. However, both of these animals have hair (around their blowholes) and give birth to live young which they suckle (feed milk). These examples can show students that classification is a science of close observation, and that we shouldn't group animals by too broad criteria.

Introduction

- Ask students if they know any other animals that they can group. (Students should say birds and fish.) Ask them: *What features would you use to group birds?* (Feathers, eggs, wings) Explain that these are similar features to the ones we use to group mammals, insects and reptiles. It is important to compare the same things when we are classifying so we can do it accurately.

- Guide students towards the group of amphibians. Ask why they think these are not reptiles. This isn't an easy question, so try to elicit from students that amphibians might reproduce differently by talking about frogs (they lay eggs in water).

- Ask students to name some fish that they know. Ask them: *Do you think a dolphin is a fish?* Explain that dolphins do live in water but that they give birth to live young which they feed with milk. Explain too that they have a small amount of hair by their blowholes and that they breathe air. Now ask the class who still thinks that dolphins are fish. Students should be guided to understand that these criteria make dolphins mammals.

Teaching and learning activities

- Ask the students to turn to pages 42 and 43 of their Student's Books. Encourage them to look at all the photographs of animals on the pages. Ask the students to name each animal.

- Once you are sure that the students can identify each animal, get them to work in their groups to answer the questions on pages 42 and 43. They can use the notes you wrote on the board to help them. Circulate and answer questions where necessary.

- The students then complete the activity on page 38 of their Workbooks. The diagram shows groups of animals. They need to list as many animals as they can in each bubble. While they are doing this, circulate and correct as necessary.

- Show the students Slideshow B6 and ask them if they can identify some of the different features that the animals have.

Biology • Topic 2 Humans and animals 2.10

Graded activities

1 Working individually, students should write down as many animals as they can and group them into the animal groups they have learned – insects, mammals, birds, reptiles, amphibians and fish.

2 Ask students to complete the boxes on page 39 of their Workbooks by drawing some animals that meet the criteria in the headings.

3 Ask students to look at the pictures of the three animals – a turtle, a duck-billed platypus and a whale. Write the names on the board. Students may need to research these animals, or you can provide them with some key information on each. They should then complete the statement at the bottom of page 39 of their Workbook.

Consolidate and review

- Give each student a copy of PCM B7, on Animal groups. Write a long list of animals on the board. The students should write the names of the animals in the correct places in the table.
- Ask students if they can add any other animals to the list. Check that any new additions are correctly placed in the table.
- Show Slideshow B7 to reinforce what the students have learned about animal groups.

Differentiation

■ All of the students should be able to sort most of the animals into groups with shared features, and explain what those shared features are.

● Most of the students will be able to give a name to the groups (birds, amphibians, fish) they create, and say what features of each animal make it a member of that group.

▲ Some of the students will be able to write down a list of criteria used to test the inclusion of an animal in a specific group and know that some features may be misleading so classification of animals must be done carefully. The duck-billed platypus is an example of this.

Biology • Topic 2 Humans and animals Consolidation

Consolidation

Student's Book page 44

Biology learning objectives

- Know life processes common to humans and animals include nutrition (water and food), movement, growth and reproduction.
- Describe differences between living and non-living things using knowledge of life processes.
- Explore and research exercise and the adequate, varied diet needed to keep healthy.
- Know that some foods can be damaging to health, e.g. very sweet and fatty foods.
- Explore human senses and the ways we use them to learn about our world.
- Sort living things into groups, using simple features and describe rationale for groupings.

Resources

- Assessment Sheets B4, B5 and B6

Classroom equipment

- coloured pens or pencils

Looking back

- Use the summary points to review the key knowledge areas students have learned in this topic. Make up some true and false statements based on the summary points. Share these with the class and let the students decide whether the statements are true or false. If they are false, they should correct the statements.
- Ask students to write down three sentences about things they have learned in this topic. Let them tell the group why they found these things interesting.

How well do you remember?

You may use the revision and consolidation activities on page 44 either as a test or as a paired class activity. If you are using the activities as a test, have the students work on their own to complete the activities in writing and then collect and mark the work. If you are using them as a class activity, you may prefer to let the students do the tasks orally. Circulate as they discuss the pictures and observe the students to see who is confident and who is unsure of the concepts.

Some suggested answers

1 They are all animals.
2 They all share the same seven life processes – respiration, growth, nutrition, movement, reproduction, sensitivity, excretion.
3 A reptiles, B birds, C mammals
4 A balanced diet, consisting of protein, carbohydrates, fruit and vegetables, and a small amount of fats and sugars.
5 Exercise to build strength, stamina and flexibility.
6 Touch, taste, sight, hearing and smell.

Assessment

A more formal assessment of the students' understanding of the topic can be undertaken using Assessment Sheets B4, B5 and B6.

Students following Cambridge Assessment International Education Primary Science Curriculum Framework will write progression tests set and supplied by Cambridge at this level and feedback will be given regarding their achievement levels.

Assessment Sheet answers

Sheet B4

1 tree, cabbage [2]
2 **Group A**   **Group B**
  bird   - can fly
  amphibian   - live near water
  mammal   - have fur
  insect   - have six legs [4]
3 eyes / nose / ears / tongue [4]

Sheet B5

1 true / false / true [3]
2 rhino / giraffe / tiger [3]
3 energy / food / protein / vegetables [4]

Sheet B6

1 Check students' statements. Possible answers could include: avoiding danger, finding food, staying safe, hearing people. [3]
2 Check students' statements. Possible answers could include: protein – milk/meat, fats – olive oil/butter, carbohydrates – bread/pasta, sugars – sweets/soda, fruit and vegetables – oranges/carrots. [5]
3 muscles / heart [2]

Student's Book answers

Pages 24–25
1. Living things – bee, pot plant. Non-living things – key, chair.
2. Reproduction – They reproduce, or have young living things like themselves.
   Nutrition – They need food and water to stay alive.
   Growth – They grow.
   Movement – They can move by themselves.
   Sensitivity – They can respond to things.
3. They can move towards sunlight.
4. To avoid danger to find food and water, to find shelter.

Pages 26–27
1. The cat and the car are living things – although the car can move, excrete (gases) and have nutrition (petrol) it can't do the other life processes.
2. One is a living lion and the other is a statue of a lion, which is non-living. The living lion breathes, eats and drinks, and moves – that's how we know it's alive.
3. No, a wooden gate is non-living. However, it was once a tree, before it was cut down and made into a gate. So it used to be a living thing.

Pages 28–29
1. Meat, fish, eggs, nuts, cheese, pulses (peas and beans), protein.
2. Carbohydrates
   They give you energy.
3. milk, fruit, cheese

Pages 30–31
1. No. Carbohydrates: potato, bread, protein – meat, fats – chips, sugars – ice cream. There are no fruits or vegetables.
2. Carbohydrates, protein, fats, sugars.
3. No. She could have vegetables instead of chips and could have an orange instead of ice cream.

Pages 32–33
1. Meat kebabs, glass of water, fruit.
2. Chips, sweets, chocolates, biscuits, fizzy drink.
3. Students' own answers. Examples include: change the cake to fresh fruit; change the chips to a salad; change the sugary drink to water.

Pages 34–35
1. Strength – being powerful, able to do many things. Flexibility – being bendy or supple. Stamina – being able to carry on doing something for a long time.
2. Strength – muscle-building exercises like sit-ups. Flexibility – stretching exercises like touching your toes. Stamina – doing an exercise regularly, like running.
3. It builds strong bones and muscles and is good for your heart (the main muscle).
4. Circulate and check students' progress.

Pages 36–37
1. So we are able to react quickly to things that happen – for example, to run away from something dangerous, to stop eating something bad.
2. touch / smell / sound / taste
3. Students' own answers. Most will answer sight, as it overrides the other senses. However, encourage students to defend and explain other answers.

Pages 38–39
1. sight
2. One person is reading braille, and the other person is using a stick to help her to find her way.
3. S/he has learned a new way of reading that uses touch. She has learned to move carefully by sensing the space ahead of her with a white stick. Compared with the way they live, my life is very easy as I can read anything, and see anything. (Students' responses will vary.)

Pages 40–41
1. They are all living things / animals. The shark has fins, the eagle has wings, and the camel has legs.
2. Limbs – legs, fins, wings. Skin – fur, scales etc. Seven life processes, especially reproduction.
3. Crocodiles, lizard – reptiles. Dolphin, horse, jerboa – mammals.
4. Six legs, hard outer shell, antennae.
5. Sense organs – smell, touch.

Pages 42–43
1. They all have limbs and similar sense organs – eyes etc.
2. Number of limbs, habitat, what they eat.
3. Clownfish, shark – they have fins and scales and live in water.
4. So they can investigate similar animals and compare groups.
5. Students' own answers, for example cats, dogs, monkeys etc.

Chemistry • Topic 3 Material properties

3.1 Properties of materials

Student's Book pages 46-47

Chemistry learning objectives
- Know that every material has specific properties e.g. hard, soft, shiny.
- Sort materials according to their properties.

Resources
- Workbook pages 40 and 41
- Slideshow C1: Materials
- PCM C1: Sorting materials
- DVD Activity C1: Metal, wood, plastic

Classroom equipment
- a house brick
- trays of objects, one tray for each group (wooden blocks, plastic rulers, metal spoons, sponges and rubber balls)
- towels for covering mystery objects
- coloured pens or pencils

Scientific enquiry skills
- *Ideas and evidence:* Collect evidence in a variety of contexts to answer questions or test ideas.
- *Plan investigative work:* Suggest ideas, make predictions and communicate these.
- *Obtain and present evidence:* Observe and compare objects, living things and events.

Key word
- texture

⚠ Remind students not to put any objects into their mouths and to be sensible with the rubber ball, as it could be a tripping hazard.

Scientific background

Materials can be classified according to their properties. There are many different properties: some are visible and some are determined by investigation or through using special equipment. The main visible properties are colour, size, shape *texture* and what it is made from. Less obvious properties include strength, hardness, permeability (how easily a gas or liquid can pass through it), porosity (how absorbent it is), buoyancy (how well it floats), flexibility and elasticity.

The properties of a material determine its suitability for a particular purpose. Often several properties are taken into consideration, including cost and availability. For example, steel is very hard and strong, but it is very dense. A material's properties can make it suitable for some uses, but unsuitable or unaffordable for others.

Introduction

- Show Slideshow C1 to introduce the topic. Summarise the presentation by saying that every material is useful in some way.

- Review some different materials from Stage 2 and list them on the board. For example, wood, steel, stone, paper, brick. Discuss the term 'properties' and explore what students think it means by asking for examples.

- Students can complete DVD Activity C1 as a revision exercise to remind them of what they have already learned in Stages 1 and 2.

- Take the brick and ask questions to explore its properties. Ask: *What colour is it? How big is it? What does it feel like?* Focus on properties that students can feel, see and smell. Explain that shape, colour, size, appearance and texture are all properties of the object. List these words on the board.

- Ask: *What words would you use to describe the properties of the brick?* (block, brown, hard) Discuss other words for the properties of different materials. List them alongside the materials.

Chemistry • Topic **3** **Material properties 3.1**

Teaching and learning activities

- Get the students to turn to page 46 in their Student's Books. Discuss the pictures briefly then let the students work in pairs to answer the questions.
- Give each group a tray with a selection of objects made from different materials. Let them examine the objects and use the descriptive words from the list on the board and the properties table on page 47 to describe the properties. Ask if they have used any words that are not on the list. Add any new words to the list on the board.
- Ask the students to group the materials according to common properties, for example, hard, soft, smooth or shiny. In each case establish which property is being used to group the materials and which objects they have chosen.

Graded activities

1 Let students look at the pictures and discuss similarities and differences in their groups. Help students to use the new vocabulary from the table in their discussion. Assess the group work.

2 Students work independently to describe their objects, using the vocabulary and the questions from the unit to help them. They record their work on page 40 of their Workbooks.

3 Students use the new vocabulary, unassisted, to describe a hidden object to their group. The group must guess what the object is. Let each student choose an object and complete the activity in their Workbooks on page 41.

Consolidate and review

- Describe your own hidden object to the class and see if the students are able to guess, by your description, what it is. When the students put up their hands, ask them which property gave them the clue to the right answer.
- Reverse the approach. Call out a property and ask students to name a material that has that property. Get a volunteer to make a list on the board of materials that share that property.
- Use the diagram on PCM C1 to check whether students are able to sort materials according to their properties.

Differentiation

■ All of the students should be able to use suitable adjectives to describe the properties of various materials. They should be able to look at objects and say what properties the objects have.

● Most of the students should be able to link the property to the descriptions being used. Most students should also be able to group different objects correctly, according to a range of properties.

▲ Some of the students should be able to write independently to describe different objects using a range of adjectives. They should be able to describe many objects accurately.

Chemistry • Topic 3 Material properties 3.2

3.2 Hard or soft?

Student's Book pages 48–49

Chemistry learning objectives
- Know that every material has specific properties e.g. hard, soft, shiny.
- Sort materials according to their properties.

Resources
- Workbook pages 42 and 43

Classroom equipment
- samples of materials for hardness testing: stone, wood, metal, plastic, rubber, polystyrene
- hard object for rub test, e.g. sandpaper or stone
- cardboard or plastic tube
- hard, heavy object, such as a stone, to drop
- small ball for hardness testing of classroom surfaces

Scientific enquiry skills
- *Ideas and evidence:* Collect evidence in a variety of contexts to answer questions or test ideas.
- *Plan investigative work:* With help, think about collecting evidence and planning fair tests.
- *Obtain and present evidence:* Observe and compare objects, living things and events.
- *Consider evidence and approach:* Draw conclusions from results and begin to use scientific knowledge to suggest explanations; make generalisations and begin to identify simple patterns in results.

Key words
- surface
- dent

⚠️ The students must take care when doing the dent test, to avoid dropping the hard object onto fingers. Assess the risk and decide on the level of supervision needed. Similar precautions will be needed for the rub test.

Scientific background

Hardness is the resistance of a material to efforts to change its shape. It can be measured by rubbing one material with another. A hard material scratches a softer one. For example, a nail scratches skin because nails are harder than skin. The hardness of a material or *surface* can be tested by a *dent* test or a rub test. To ensure reliable results, the test must be fair. This means that everything should be kept the same except for one element (the variable). In this instance, the only thing that should change is the material being dented or rubbed. Note that hardness is not the same as strength, which will be explore in the next unit.

Introduction

- Point out some examples of hard materials from around the classroom (for example, metal, glass, wood and plastic). Give the students time to look and make the connections between the objects.
- Now ask about soft materials (for example cotton, rubber, paper) and ask individuals for their ideas about the properties of these materials.
- Now show two similar materials, such as two different metals. Ask: *Which one is harder?* This is a much more difficult comparison. Say that sometimes it is difficult to tell which material is harder so we need to do a test.
- Direct the students to page 48 of the Student's Book. Encourage them to talk about the pictures and identify which materials and surfaces are hard and which are soft.
- Read through the questions with the students and let them discuss their answers with a partner. Take feedback.

Teaching and learning activities

- Ask the students to look at the diagrams of the rub test and the dent test on page 49. Show them how these experiments test for hardness. Use the equipment at the front of the class to demonstrate the tests.

- Rub test: Rub an object (such as a stone or a sandpaper block) over the material being tested. Stress to students that they must rub the material in the same direction, with the same pressure, each time, to make it a fair test. If the object scratches the material being rubbed, the material is softer than the object.
- Dent test: Drop an object through the tube, onto the material being tested. Remind the class about fair testing and the need to drop the object from the same height each time. If the object dents the material, the material is softer. If the material is not dented, then it is harder than the object.
- Now let the students do the tests. Give each pair a cardboard tube, an object to drop, and a selection of materials to investigate. Tell them to use the rub then dent test to find out which of their materials is the hardest. They should record their results in their Workbooks on page 42.
- When they have completed the rub test, they should do the dent test.

Graded activities

1 Students work individually to think of two substances that need to be hard and two substances that need to be soft. They should write them down and explain why these need to be harder or softer. If you feel students need peer support you can let them discuss this in pairs first before doing the activity.

2 Students record the results of the rub test and the dent test in their Workbooks on pages 42 and 43. Although the practical part of this activity is group work, the recording of results should be done individually.

3 Students should test other surfaces in the classroom and report back to the class. They should not test by denting or rubbing, but rather by bouncing a small ball on the surfaces, or finding another way to test for hardness.

Consolidate and review

- Ask the students to report back to the class on the results of their tests on other surfaces. Ask them to group the materials they tested into hard and soft. Ask: *Does everyone agree? Which materials are the hardest? Which are the softest?*
- List common hard and soft materials on the board in two columns. Before you write each word, ask: *Which column should this go into? Why do you say so? Why does this substance need to be hard/soft?*

Differentiation

■ All of the students should be able to name two or three hard materials, such as wood, brick or stone. They should be able to name two or three soft materials, such as fabric, foam and carpet.

● Most of the students should be able to explain how to make these tests fair, by dropping the same object from the same height, or rubbing in the same direction with the same pressure.

▲ Some of the students should be able to suggest ways of investigating other surfaces without using the rub or dent tests.

Chemistry • Topic **3** Material properties 3.3

3.3 Strength

Student's Book pages 50–51
Chemistry learning objectives
- Know that every material has specific properties e.g. hard, soft, shiny.
- Sort materials according to their properties.
- Discuss why materials are chosen for specific purposes on the basis of their properties.

Resources
- Workbook page 44
- PCM C2: Strong or weak?
- DVD Activity C2: Hardness and strength

Classroom equipment
- a paper bag and a plastic bag
- wide strips of cotton, wool, fleece, plastic, wood (ruler), steel (bar), rope (natural) and elastic
- loads with equal mass (e.g. marbles)
- plastic containers
- sticky tape and small pieces of string

Scientific enquiry skills
- *Ideas and evidence:* Collect evidence in a variety of contexts to answer questions or test ideas.
- *Plan investigative work:* Suggest ideas, make predictions and communicate these; with help, think about collecting evidence and planning fair tests.
- *Obtain and present evidence:* Measure using simple equipment and record observations in a variety of ways; present results in drawings, bar charts and tables.
- *Consider evidence and approach:* Draw conclusions from results and begin to use scientific knowledge to suggest explanations.

Key words
- **strong**
- **load**

> ⚠ Provide the students with eye protection to protect against items which are being extended or snapped. Put a large box on the floor to catch the weights. Advise the students to take care not to drop the load onto their fingers or the floor. Assess the risk and decide the level of supervision needed for individuals.

Scientific background

The *stronger* a material is, the more stress it can withstand, the heavier the *load* it can carry and the harder it is to break when being stretched. Some materials are stronger than others and are used for different purposes. Note that strength is not the same as hardness. Something can be hard but not very strong, or strong but not very hard. A rope, for instance, is strong but not hard – you can cut through it easily but it can lift a heavy load without breaking.

Introduction

- Review the last activity from the previous lesson. Encourage students to use the correct terminology to describe the surfaces they tested. Explain that they have looked at how hard surfaces are; now they are going to look at how strong surfaces are.

- Show the students two bags, one made of paper and one made of plastic. Ask: *Which bag is stronger?* Ask individuals to respond, and to explain how they know. Explain that if you put too much in the paper bag, you have too much of a load and it will break easily. The paper bag is not designed to carry a heavy load. The plastic bag has been designed to carry a heavier load for longer.

- Get students to look at the pictures in the Student's Book on page 50. Ask: *What has happened? What would you tell the person with the shopping?* Read through the questions with the students then let them discuss their answers with a partner.

50

Chemistry • Topic 3 Material properties 3.3

Teaching and learning activities

- Explain that students are going to test some natural and some made materials, to see which are stronger. Take a class vote on the issue first and write the predictions on the board. Go through each prediction and ask the students why they made that prediction.
- Set up the equipment as shown in the diagram in the Students' Book. Show the students what to do, starting with the lightest load and adding to it. Say that they will be testing strips of different natural and made materials. Show them the way to connect the load properly, making sure it is suspended above the floor, hanging from the material they are testing.
- Remind them that the test must be fair, so the strips must be the same size. Stress that they must make sure the loads are attached properly and that the investigation ends when the material being tested is broken, not when the load falls off. If the load is not fixed securely, it may fall off without the material breaking.

Graded activities

As this is a practical investigation, it is recommended that the students work in mixed ability groups for this activity. Differentiation should be through the level of support the students receive as they work on the activity, as well as by outcome (please see guidance in the 'Differentiation' box right).

1 Students work in their groups to set up the equipment correctly. Circulate and check that they are making the test fair by using strips of the same length, and loads of the same weight. Make sure that they use the equipment safely and help any who are finding it difficult to carry their loads.

2 Students record the results of their tests individually in their Workbooks on page 44.

3 Ask students individually to investigate other materials in the classroom. They should rank the materials in order from weakest to strongest, recording their results on PCM C2.

Consolidate and review

- Ask the students to share the information they gathered from the other materials in the classroom. How many students have similar items on the list? What are they? Who has tested something unusual? Where does it fit on the scale of hardness?
- Explain that a friend of yours wants to hang up a heavy object. Can the class suggest three natural and three made materials your friend should try? Ask the students to predict which material will be the strongest and which will be the weakest. Ask students to describe a simple experiment your friend could do to test the materials. How would you make the test fair? Take individual responses from students about the best materials to use. Ask the students to give you reasons for choosing each material.
- Let the students complete DVD Activity C2 to consolidate what they have learned about hardness and strength.

Differentiation

■ All of the students should be able to suggest some strong natural and some strong human-made materials. They should be able to suggest ways to make the test fair and be able to set up the experiment with little or no help.

● Most of the students should be able to describe ways to test the materials. They should be able to record the results of their fair test with little or no help.

▲ Some of the students should be able to rank the materials in order from weakest to strongest using knowledge they have gained in this topic.

Chemistry • Topic 3 Material properties 3.4

3.4 Flexibility

Student's Book pages 52–53
Chemistry learning objectives
- Know that every material has specific properties e.g. hard, soft, shiny.
- Sort materials according to their properties.
- Discuss why materials are chosen for specific purposes on the basis of their properties.

Resources
- Workbook pages 45, 46 and 47
- PCM C3: How flexible?

Classroom equipment
- selection of flexible and non-flexible objects, e.g. rubber bands, balloons etc.
- identical lengths of wood, plastic, metal and card
- sticky tape, string and some weights
- coloured pens or pencils

Scientific enquiry skills
- *Ideas and evidence:* Collect evidence in a variety of contexts to answer questions or test ideas.
- *Plan investigative work:* Suggest ideas, make predictions and communicate these.
- *Obtain and present evidence:* Observe and compare objects, living things and events; present results in drawings, bar charts and tables.

Key words
- **stretchiness**
- **rigid**

⚠️ Remind students that they must take care when letting go of stretched materials, and not to drop weights onto their fingers or the floor.

Scientific background

Some materials can be altered by being squashed or bent but others cannot. These changes can be either *reversible* (can be changed back) or *irreversible* (cannot be changed back). Using forces such as pushing, pulling and twisting, we can investigate different materials to find out how squashy and bendy they are. A material that is very squashy and bendy is called a *flexible* material. A material that is cannot be squashed or bent is called a *rigid* material.

Most airplanes have an emergency flotation device (life jacket) under each seat. In an emergency, these can be inflated by the passengers. If the plane comes down on water, the emergency doors open and an inflatable slide is let down. The passengers slide down this, and once they reach the water they are able to float safely in their life jackets. The life jackets and slides must be made of very flexible material, so that they can be blown up quickly. They also need to be strong, so they do not burst under impact.

Introduction

- Review the properties of materials that students have investigated so far. Make sure that students understand the terms 'hard' and 'soft', and 'strong' and 'weak'. Have a spot check by asking random students to identify things in the classroom that have these properties. You could also divide the class in half and have a quick quiz.
- Get students to complete the table on page 45 of the Workbook. Ask them to select the most important property for the object to do its job, and to suggest a suitable material. They should say why they have chosen this material rather than another.
- Once you are sure that the whole class has grasped these concepts, move on to a discussion of a new property: flexibility.
- Ask students if they know what the term 'flexible' means. Accept all answers that use words like *stretchy* or bendy. Ask for examples of flexible materials that they know. Accept answers like elastic, clay, rubber bands, and hair ties. Some students might remember flexibility from the unit on exercise in Topic 2.

Chemistry • Topic 3 Material properties 3.4

Teaching and learning activities

- Ask students to look at the picture on page 52 of the Student's Book. Discuss the questions with the class. Talk about other objects that are flexible and that return to their original shape once you stop stretching them.
- Now talk about the life jacket on page 53 of the Student's Book. Ask the class if anyone has used a life jacket in the water before. Ask: *How did you inflate it? What happened when you let the air out? What material was the life jacket made of? Why was it made of this material?* Invite answers to the questions on page 53 of the Student's Book.

Graded activities

1 Each student should take a turn to identify one object in the classroom that is made of a flexible material and say why it is made of that material. You can give the class five minutes to work individually on this, before reporting back to their group.

Ask students to identify an object in the classroom that needs to be rigid. Now ask students to think further and imagine what would happen to the object if it was not made of a rigid material.

2 Give each group a selection of flexible and non-flexible objects. Ask students to sort the objects into those that can bend and those that cannot bend. Then ask students to rank the objects that can bend in order from most flexible to least flexible, with 1 being the least flexible and 4 the most flexible.

Encourage shared class discussion. Which groups have the same collection of flexible objects? Which groups have the same order of flexibility? Has any group got an unusual order? Students can write their predictions and their findings into their Workbooks on page 46.

3 Students should work in their group to test various substances for flexibility. Get them to set up the experiment themselves, using PCM C3. Warn them about the danger of dropping weights and hurting themselves. Circulate and assist where needed.

Consolidate and review

- Remind students about the airbag they learned about in Stage 2. If necessary, revisit the airbag topic quickly. What properties does it share with a life jacket? What kind of material are both of these life-saving devices made of? Start a class discussion on other inflatable devices (for example, lilos for swimming pools, rubber boats, arm bands etc.)
- Have a quick test. Ask students to write down the names of as many flexible *objects* as they can think of in one minute. Who has the longest list?
- Now ask students to write down the names of as many flexible *materials* as they can think of in one minute (cotton, nylon, elastic etc.). You can extend this activity by writing all the answers on the board and then dividing them into natural and made materials.
- Students can do the activity on page 47 of the Workbook. The task is to fill in the missing words and to design and draw a life jacket.

Differentiation

■ All of the students should be able to name some flexible materials and rank them in order of flexibility. They should also be able to suggest uses for flexible materials and explain why certain objects are made of these materials.

● Most of the students should be able to test and rank the materials in order of flexibility with little or no help.

▲ Some of the students should be able to explain why certain objects need to be made of flexible materials and suggest what would happen if they were made out of rigid materials instead.

Chemistry • Topic 3 Material properties 3.5

3.5 Structures

Student's Book pages 54–55

Chemistry learning objectives
- Know that every material has specific properties e.g. hard, soft, shiny.
- Discuss why materials are chosen for specific purposes on the basis of their properties.

Resources
- Workbook pages 48 and 49
- PCM C4: Does shape affect strength?

Classroom equipment
- sticky tape or glue
- scissors
- suitable weights to test the strength of the structures
- coloured pens or pencils

Scientific enquiry skills
- *Ideas and evidence:* Collect evidence in a variety of contexts to answer questions or test ideas.
- *Plan investigative work:* Suggest ideas, make predictions and communicate these.
- *Obtain and present evidence:* Observe and compare objects, living things and events.
- *Consider evidence and approach:* Make generalisations and begin to identify simple patterns in results.

Key words
- **stable**
- **collapse**

⚠ Supervise the students when they use scissors. If you take the students on a walk, ensure they are safe and that they stay together.

Scientific background

Although some materials share properties (for example, hardness) they are not all equally useful. A hard material such as stone makes a strong structure when used as part of an arch or dome. However, stone would not be useful in building a boat, because it is too heavy. Wood is relatively hard, but it can be crafted into different shapes, and it is slightly flexible, so it is good for flooring, or roof trusses.

Some shapes are inherently strong. A triangle cannot change shape unless the components are deformed. That is why triangles are used in bridges, to maintain the shape and so that they do not collapse.

When designing a building or structure, architects and engineers consider many factors, including all of the outside forces – the *pushes* and *pulls* – that the structure may encounter. Weather and other natural forces, such as earthquakes, can apply *stress* to structures. Certain shapes, such as rectangles, circles, squares and triangles, are stronger than others depending on the way that these forces affect them. A shape that distributes a force equally along all of its sides is especially *stable*.

Introduction

- Ask the class what they think 'strong' means. Ask: *What makes something strong? Can you give me examples of strong structures?* Ask the class what they think 'stable' means. Ask: *What makes something stable? Can you give me examples of stable structures?*

- Ask the students to try and balance their pencils on end on their desks. Are they able to do it? Ask them what they could do to make their pencils more stable. Explain that something is stable if it can stay in the same position without being knocked over.

- Let the students investigate ways to make their pencils stable. They can use their erasers, books, lunchboxes etc. to provide buttressing. Look around for the most innovative construction. Walk around the class, pointing out the different solutions that students have found.

Chemistry • Topic 3 Material properties 3.5

Teaching and learning activities

- Ask students to look at the photograph of the bridge on page 54 of the Student's Book. Ask them what material it is made of. Ask: *Why do you think the builders used that material?* Ask them to identify different shapes in the structure. Ask: *Why do you think the builders used these shapes?*
- Talk about other uses for metal and for wood. Make a list on the board of all the ideas the students have, under the headings 'wood' and 'metal'.
- Now ask the students, in their groups, to make a list of all the shapes they see in the buildings around them. You may want to allow them to do this in the school grounds, or even in the area around the school, on a school outing.
- Discuss the photograph of the city on page 55 of the Student's Book. Talk about the questions and allow students to be imaginative. Direct their attention to the fact that buildings with a wider base are more stable than tall thin buildings. Ask: *Which is the tallest building you know? How do you think the builders made it stable? Which is the most stable building you know? Why do you consider it to be very stable?*

Graded activities

1 Students should work in their groups to identify all the objects made from metal and from wood in their classroom. They should write down why metal or wood was used to make each object. They should try and find at least five objects for each material.

2 Use the nets on PCM C4 for the shape-testing activity. Each student should have a copy of PCM C4, a pair of scissors, and glue or sticky tape to build the nets into 3D shapes. Once the shapes are built, get the students to test them with different weights or different forces (they can simulate a hurricane, for example). Remind them that their tests should be fair. Students should record the results of their fair tests on the different shapes in their Workbooks on page 48.

3 Students should research the materials and shapes that builders use in hurricane areas. They can complete the activity on page 49 of their Workbooks.

Consolidate and review

- Take feedback from each group after they return from their short outing to collect information about the shapes of buildings. How many shapes has each group recorded? Is there a common shape for most big buildings? What conclusion do they reach about the way most buildings are structured?
- Ask the students about the shapes they built from the nets. Ask: *What was difficult about this activity? What was easy?* Find out which shape they had the most trouble making. Ask for their opinions about which of the nets produced the most stable shape.
- Review Activity 3, asking students to stand up and show the class their researched pictures or drawings of different buildings designed to withstand hurricanes. Discuss what they found out. Ask them about the materials used in each building.

Differentiation

■ All of the students should be able to independently identify materials made from wood and from metal in the classroom and say why that material was used.

● Most of the students should be able to say why certain shapes are used in buildings. Most students understand that certain shapes and construction techniques are used to make buildings strong and stable.

▲ Some of the students should be able to suggest why materials are used in buildings that they have not seen themselves. They can take their knowledge and apply it to an unknown building, which has to be built to meet certain weather conditions.

Chemistry • Topic 3 Material properties 3.6

3.6 Uses of materials

Student's Book pages 56–57

Chemistry learning objective
- Discuss why materials are chosen for specific purposes on the basis of their properties.

Resources
- Workbook page 50
- PCM C5: Building materials
- Slideshow C2: Properties of materials

Classroom equipment
- a selection of classroom objects made from different materials
- a picture of a family car
- access to computers with graphics software (optional)
- flashcards to show (separately) the words 'properties', 'materials' and 'purposes', and their meanings

Scientific enquiry skills
- *Plan investigative work:* Suggest ideas, make predictions and communicate these.
- *Obtain and present evidence:* Observe and compare objects, living things and events.

Key words
- purpose
- construct

Scientific background

Students have been learning about properties of materials and should be able to draw the conclusion that certain materials have properties which make them suitable for different *purposes*. Materials can be hard, soft, strong, weak, flexible, transparent etc. When objects are made, they are made using materials that suit their purpose. For example, spectacles are made from transparent glass or plastic, bridges are *constructed* from steel girders to make them strong, and bricks are made from hard, porous clay. All materials have more than one property, so architects, builders and manufacturers have to consider what the most important property is that they need. Sometimes it is not the property of the material that determines whether it is used in an object or not, but its cost. Gold is a hard material but you could not afford to make a car out of it.

Introduction

- Begin by identifying various objects in the classroom or the playground. Ask: *What is that object? What is its purpose? What material is it made from? Why is it made from that material?*

- Let students work in groups to identify objects from their descriptions. Each student should write down a description of an object and then the rest of the group should guess what he or she is describing. The objects do not have to be limited to the near environment.

- Students should then explain why they think that object is made from a certain material. What properties does it need?

Teaching and learning activities

- Students can work in pairs if you feel they need peer support for this activity; otherwise it can be done individually.

- Look at the picture of the house on page 56 of the Student's Books. The students should answer the questions and should think about the way that certain materials are more suitable than others.

- Once the students have completed the questions, let them discuss their answers in their groups and then present their findings as a group response. You should circulate while the groups are combining their information, to make sure that everyone is getting a chance to contribute, and that group-work rules are being adhered to.

Chemistry • Topic 3 Material properties 3.6

- Now direct students to the pictures on page 57 of their Student's Book. This introduces the idea of multiple properties and makes students think about what the dominant property is. They should look at the pictures and answer the questions, either in groups or individually.
- Show the class Slideshow C2 and discuss why the different materials have been used in each picture. Is it because they are hard or soft, rigid or flexible, etc?

Graded activities

1 Show the students the picture of a family car, and ask them to think about all the parts of a car they know. They should write the name, or ask you the name, of each part and then explain what material they think it is made of and why. Students can complete the table on page 50 of their Workbooks.

2 The students should design a 'house of the future'. They can use any materials they want, but they must say what properties each material has which make it suitable for the job. Let the students work individually to complete this task. If you have access to computers and graphics software then this activity could be done digitally and presented as a slideshow to the rest of the class.

3 The students should use the knowledge they have gained so far in this topic to invent a new material that has more than one useful property. They should describe what it could be used for. For example, a material that is as hard as metal but as flexible as paper could be used for making storage boxes. The new material must have a practical application in the real world.

Consolidate and review

- Check that the students know the difference between the word 'property' and the term 'purpose'. The one is something a material has and the other is something a material does, or can do.
- Ask different students what materials they are wearing or what materials they are sitting on. Then ask their partner to say why the material is suited to its specific purpose.

- Revise the important terms 'properties', 'materials' and 'purposes', by cutting out flashcards of the words and flashcards of their meanings. Students can match the words to their meanings.
- Use PCM C5 to make three sets of flashcards, showing different materials, their properties and their uses.
- Students need to match up the cards into the correct sets of three cards.

Differentiation

■ All of the students should be able to identify and name most of the materials used to make a car. They should be able to write a short explanation stating why those particular materials have been used in relation to their properties.

● Most of the students should be able to design a futuristic house using their knowledge of the properties of materials they have gained in this topic. Less able students may design houses that are unstable, or use materials which are unsuitable; guide them towards choosing more suitable materials and structures.

▲ Some of the students should be able to use their knowledge of material properties to invent some interesting and useful new materials. This activity allows the students to stretch themselves intellectually and to apply their knowledge creatively.

Chemistry • Topic 3 Material properties 3.7

3.7 Staying the same shape

Student's Book pages 58–59

Chemistry learning objectives
- Know that every material has specific properties, e.g. hard, soft, shiny.
- Sort materials according to their properties.
- Discuss why materials are chosen for specific purposes on the basis of their properties.

Resources
- Workbook page 51
- PCM C6: Elastic materials

Classroom equipment
- tennis or squash ball
- loops made from a variety of elastic materials, e.g. rubber bands, hair ties, tights, elastic bandage, rope, rubber gloves
- small weights
- eye protection

Scientific enquiry skills
- *Ideas and evidence:* Collect evidence in a variety of contexts to answer questions or test ideas.
- *Plan investigative work:* Suggest ideas, make predictions and communicate these; with help, think about collecting evidence and planning fair tests.
- *Obtain and present evidence:* Observe and compare objects, living things and events; measure using simple equipment and record observations in a variety of ways.

Key words
- elastic
- original

⚠️ Warn students to take care to avoid being hit when stretchy materials snap back to their original shape. They should wear eye protection throughout the elasticity testing.

Scientific background

Some materials are *elastic* – they can be stretched but will return to their *original* shape once the force has been removed. Materials are either elastic or they are inelastic and rigid. The fabric that is called 'elastic' is not the only material that has this property. Many other materials have elastic properties to greater or lesser extents. Materials with these properties are used for many things, from clothes to car tyres.

Introduction

- Remind students that they learned about flexible materials in Unit 3.4. Ask them if they can name some flexible materials. Ask: *Who can remember what the opposite of 'flexible' is?* Then ask students to give you examples of rigid materials.
- Bounce a squash ball or a tennis ball on the classroom floor. Ask: *What am I doing? Why is the ball able to bounce?* When someone uses the word 'flexible' say 'yes' and explain that the ball is made of a flexible material, but it is also an elastic material.

- Demonstrate with a rubber band. Show how, with both the ball and the band, the object returns to its original shape after being stretched. You may want to push down on the ball on a desk to demonstrate the way that it changes shape and then returns to its original shape when released. Ask if students know of any other objects or substances that are elastic. Make sure they know the difference between the physical property 'elasticity' and the materials in the things we call elastic bands.

Teaching and learning activities

- Ask the students to study the pictures in the Student's Book on page 58. Talk about which of the materials need to stretch the most and which need to stretch the least. Ask: *If the boy's top were made of a rigid material, like canvas, would he be able to lift his arm? Why is it useful to wear stretchy clothes when playing sport?*
- Let students investigate the qualities of their own clothes. Which items are the most elastic, and why do they need to be elastic? (shoe soles, hair ties etc.) Which items are least elastic, and why do these need to be more rigid? (hats, shoe uppers etc.)

Chemistry • Topic 3 Material properties 3.7

- Get students to discuss the objects in the pictures on page 59 in their groups. They should use the questions on page 58 to guide their discussion.

Graded activities

1 In their groups, the students should discuss which items are most and least elastic, and why each item needs the property of elasticity. Once the group discussion is over, let students record their ranking order in their exercise books.

2 Each group tests a selection of materials with elastic properties. First demonstrate the experiment to them, following the instructions on PCM C6. Let them set up the investigation on their own. Circulate while the groups are working, offering assistance where necessary. Make sure that the students are wearing eye protection throughout the experiment, even when their own group is not testing the materials. Check that each test is fair by making sure that the students correctly line up each loop with the mark on the wall, that they are using weights of equal mass, and that they are measuring the distance between the correct pair of marks each time. Students should make predictions beforehand and then record their findings in their Workbooks on page 51.

3 Students should carry out research individually on a material with elastic properties that interests them. They should report back to the class in a formal oral presentation.

Consolidate and review

- Circulate round the class when students are discussing the elastic properties of the objects in the Student's Book and assess how well the group discussion is going. Is everyone getting a chance to speak? Are different opinions being respected? Do students wait their turn or are they interrupting each other? Give feedback to each group as an informal star rating.

- Check each student's exercise book, to see if they have been able to record the materials in order of elasticity. Discuss errors individually with the students who have not been able to rank the objects in the correct order.

- Assess each student presentation from Activity 3. Students must present their report in front of the class. Give marks for interest, good examples, extra effort, visual aids and fluency of delivery.

Differentiation

■ All of the students should be able to identify objects that are elastic and say why this property is useful. They should be able to rank the objects from most stretchy to least stretchy, although their rankings may not always agree. Less able students should be encouraged to accept that this ranking is not the result of a scientific test, but is more subjective. To find the objects' actual elasticity, a fair test would need to be carried out.

● Most of the students should be able to explain what you should keep the same when testing for elasticity. They should be able to set up the investigation with little or no help and be able to independently record their results.

▲ Some students should be able to take their knowledge and apply it to an unknown material, and will be able to present an interesting presentation about a different elastic material, which shares the properties they have learned about in class.

Chemistry • Topic 3 Material properties 3.8

3.8 Floating or sinking?

Student's Book pages 60–61

Chemistry learning objectives
- Know that every material has specific properties, e.g. hard, soft, shiny.
- Sort materials according to their properties.

Resources
- Workbook pages 52 and 53
- PCM C7: Will it float?
- DVD Activity C3: Will it float?

Classroom equipment
- large transparent container and fizzy water
- raisins, and other small objects such as rice grains, maize kernels etc.
- aluminium foil
- examples of the objects shown on pages 60 and 61 of the Student's Book (or other suitable objects)
- sheets of paper
- scissors, and glue or sticky tape
- basins half-full of water
- small weights of equal mass, e.g. small coins
- coloured pens or pencils

Scientific enquiry skills
- *Ideas and evidence:* Collect evidence in a variety of contexts to answer questions or test ideas.
- *Plan investigative work:* Suggest ideas, make predictions and communicate these.
- *Obtain and present evidence:* Observe and compare objects, living things and events; measure using simple equipment and record observations in a variety of ways.
- *Consider evidence and approach:* Draw conclusions from results and begin to use scientific knowledge to suggest explanations.

Key words
- **float**
- **sink**

⚠️ Remind students to take care with water spillages. Mop them up immediately to avoid slipping. Supervise the students when they use scissors.

Scientific background

When an object is placed in a liquid, it moves the liquid out of its way. This is called *displacement*. An object will *sink* if it weighs more than the liquid it displaces, and it will *float* if it weighs less than the liquid it displaces.

Shapes help an object to float. A ball of clay will sink, but a model canoe made from the same amount of clay can float because it pushes more fluid out of the way, in relation to its weight. Boats can float despite the heavy and dense materials used to build them because of the large amount of air inside the hull. Hollow objects are able to float better than solid objects.

Introduction

- Tell the students that most objects either float or sink, but that you are going to show them some objects that seem to do both.

- Fill a large basin with fizzy water. Drop a few raisins into the water. They will sink, but then come back up to the surface again. Ask: *What is happening? Why is this happening? Are the raisins floating or sinking?*

- Explain that the bubbles in the water attach themselves to the raisins and lift them to the surface. You can try this with other small objects, like grains of rice, or maize kernels. Establish that air helps to make things float. Ask: *How could this be used in real life?*

- Encourage students to think about what makes some objects float and some objects sink. Make a model boat out of aluminium foil. Show students that it floats, even though it is made of metal. Ask them why they think the boat floats. Establish that, as well as air, the shapes of objects can help them to float. A big metal boat is full of air, and has special tanks full of air on each side, inside the boat, called ballasts.

Chemistry • Topic 3 Material properties 3.8

Teaching and learning activities

- Ask students to look at the pictures on pages 60 and 61 of their Student's Books and work through the questions.
- In groups, students should make predictions about which of the objects will float and which will sink. They should then test the objects safely to see whether their predictions were correct.
- Let the students test their boats from Activity 2 in a basin half-full of water. Ask: *Which one floats the best? Why do you think it floats best?*
- Ask students to pick two of the most successful boats and see how much weight they can take before they start sinking. You can do this by adding coins to the boats, one coin at a time. Use the same coins for each to ensure that this is a fair test.
- Discuss what happened as a class. Ask: *Which boats floated the best? What did they have in common? Which material floated the best?* (Materials that absorb water easily will make poor floaters.)

Graded activities

As this is a practical investigation, it is recommended that the students work in mixed ability groups for this activity. Differentiation should be through the level of support the students receive as they work on the activity, as well as by outcome (please see guidance in the 'Differentiation' box bottom right).

1 The students should create a table and write in their predictions based on whether or not they think an object will float or sink. If you do not have the objects in the pictures available for them to test, then substitute them with any others that are suitable. Let the students discuss in their groups whether their predictions were correct.

2 The students should build the boats in the pictures, using PCM C7 as a guide, and test them to see which ones float the best. They should be able to see that the boats which contain the most air float the best.

Students write their own plan for making their boats float better. This could include changing the material used and/or the shape of the boat. They should then build and test their modified boats. They should be prepared to stand up and explain their plan, and whether or not it worked, to the class. Let the class speculate about why different plans did or did not work.

3 Now ask students to design their own oil tanker. They should draw and label the oil tanker in their Workbooks on page 52. They should also provide a list of the materials used and explain how the tanker floats.

Consolidate and review

- Copy the table from page 53 of the Workbook on the board. Now ask the class to choose five objects and write them in column 1 of your table. Ask what material each object is made of, and fill in the answers in column 2. Then get the class to predict which of the objects will float and which will sink. Write down the predictions in column 3. Finally, test each object in a basin of water, and write the result in column 4. The class can copy down the work as you go. Ask students to complete their own tables for different objects on page 53 of their Workbooks.
- Assess whether each student has been able to design an oil tanker, give a list of materials, and explain why and how the tanker will float.
- Let the students complete DVD Activity C3 to say if the different objects will float or sink in water.

Differentiation

■ All of the students should be able to predict and then test the different objects to see which will float and which will sink. This activity is not difficult and should be used to introduce the concept of floating and sinking to the students.

● Most of the students should be able to construct the paper boats by following the instructions supplied. They will be able to say which shapes floated best. Less able students may need some additional help when writing their plans for making the boats float better.

▲ All of the students should be able to select suitable materials and give an appropriate design for an oil tanker. Most of the students should be able to write descriptions of the materials and shapes they have used. Some of the students should be able to explain why they have chosen particular materials and shapes for their tankers. They have recognised the need for air to make the tanker lighter.

Chemistry • Topic 3 Material properties 3.9

3.9 See-through or not?

Student's Book pages 62–63
Chemistry learning objectives
- Know that every material has specific properties, e.g. hard, soft, shiny.
- Sort materials according to their properties.
- Discuss why materials are chosen for specific purposes, based on their properties.

Resources
- Workbook page 54
- Slideshow C3: Glass buildings

Classroom equipment
- a selection of bottles, ranging from transparent, through translucent, to opaque
- glass and plastic bottles or jars
- sheets of paper, plastic, fabric and plywood

Scientific enquiry skills
- *Plan investigative work:* Suggest ideas, make predictions and communicate these.
- *Obtain and present evidence:* Observe and compare objects, living things and events.

Key words
- see-through
- cloudy

⚠ Warn students to be careful when handling glass bottles, as they could break. They should also watch out for the sharp edges on plastic bottle tops.

Scientific background

Glass is an unusual material. It is made from sand, sodium carbonate and limestone, heated to a high temperature and cooled. It is sometimes called a *super-cooled liquid*, but a more accurate description is an *amorphous solid.* This means the particles are in set positions, but, unlike most solids, the arrangement of the particles is not regular. They are arranged much as in a liquid, but (unlike a liquid) do not move around, except over hundreds of years.

The property of *transparency* refers to letting light through. This means that the light rays pass through an object without being changed in any way by the material they pass through. Glass, some plastics, air and water have this property.

Materials are transparent (see-through), translucent (*cloudy*) or opaque (not see-through), depending on how much light they allow through. Translucent materials allow some light to pass through, but not all. Looking through these materials, you can see a blurred outline. They are used, for example, in bathroom windows, as they give some privacy. Opaque materials block the light totally. These materials create dark shadows. Some bottles are opaque to protect the substance inside from light.

Introduction

- Ask the students to talk in pairs about the many different uses of glass that they can think of. They should make a list of glass objects and what they are used for. Then take feedback from the class.
- Ask the students to look at the different uses of glass that they have come up with, and decide what properties of glass give it so many uses. Establish that glass is see-through.
- Ask: *Is all glass see-through?* Encourage students to find examples of glass that is not. If they need help, mention bathroom windows, olive oil bottles or the glass panes on some front doors. Ask: *Why is it sometimes useful for glass not to be see-though?* Encourage answers that mention privacy for window or glass door panels and protection of the contents for some bottled substances.

Chemistry • Topic 3 Material properties 3.9

Teaching and learning activities

- Show the students Slideshow C3, which shows buildings in the world made from glass. Ask: *Why do you think glass is used in this way? What properties of glass are being used in these buildings?*

- Direct the students to the large picture on page 62 of their Student's Books. In pairs, ask them to read through and answer the questions. Select different students to respond to the questions in class.

- Introduce the terms 'cloudy', 'see-through' and 'not see-through'. Write the three terms on the board. Ask questions about objects you have in the classroom and then get volunteers to write the name of each object under the correct term. Ask: *Is your lunchbox see-through? Is the window cloudy? Is the table not see-through?* etc.

- Get the students to look at the pictures on page 63 of their Student's Books and work in pairs to answer the questions.

Graded activities

1 Students study the pictures of the bottles on page 63. If you are able to, bring in real bottles for this activity so that the students can handle the bottles and see what the contents are. The students should sort the bottles into groups and give reasons why each bottle allows all, some or no light into it. Perfumes need to be protected from light and heat or they will go off. Olive oil goes rancid when exposed to light and heat so it is usually stored in a cloudy (translucent) bottle.

2 Students should do some research on their own about glass and plastic bottles, and write down their findings. Plastic bottles don't break, which is a huge advantage and is why they are used for babies' bottles and soft drinks. Plastic is also less expensive than glass, so manufacturers often choose it for cost reasons. Glass can be recycled and is more environmentally friendly. Some plastics can also be recycled.

3 Various materials can be tested to see which one makes a good window blind. First get students to establish what one needs in a window blind. Must it block all the light? Must it block only some of the light? Have a range of materials on hand for testing: sheets of paper, plastic, fabric and plywood. The students should set up a fair test and then write their findings in their Workbooks on page 54.

Consolidate and review

- Have a quick class quiz. Ask ten questions such as: *Is wood see-through? What does cloudy mean? Write down one not see-through substance. Why do we use plastic for babies' bottles? Are perfume bottles see-through?* This quick quiz will give you a very good idea of which students have, or have not, mastered the new key terms.

- Get students to design and draw a bottle to hold a substance of their choice. They should label the bottle, say how much light it allows in, and explain why they have chosen to make the bottle translucent, etc.

Differentiation

■ All of the students should be able to sort the bottles into see-through, cloudy and not see-through. They may need help, or some additional information, to say why certain materials use see-through, cloudy or not see-through containers. Accept any reasonable explanations.

● Most of the students should be able to evaluate the properties of plastic and glass for making bottles, and give advantages and disadvantages of each material.

▲ Some of the students should be able to to suggest a variety of different materials which would be suitable to make a window blind. The important factor is that the blind should not be see-through; it should block the light. They will be able to independently test materials and complete page 54 in their Workbooks with little or no help.

Chemistry • Topic 3 Material properties 3.10

3.10 Wet or dry?

Student's Book pages 64–65

Chemistry learning objectives
- Know that every material has specific properties, e.g. hard, soft, shiny.
- Sort materials according to their properties.
- Discuss why materials are chosen for specific purposes on the basis of their properties.

Resources
- Workbook pages 55 and 56
- DVD Activity C4: Will the water stay out?

Classroom equipment
- range of absorbent materials, such as kitchen roll, toilet paper, towels
- range of non-absorbent materials, such as wood, metal and stone

Scientific enquiry skills
- *Plan investigative work:* Suggest ideas, make predictions and communicate these; with help, think about collecting evidence and planning fair tests.
- *Obtain and present evidence:* Observe and compare objects, living things and events.

Key words
- soak
- absorbent
- waterproof

⚠ Remind students to take care with water spillages. Mop them up immediately to avoid slipping. Check that students' plans are safe before letting them carry out their tests.

Scientific background

Some materials *soak* up liquid when they come into contact with it. These materials are *absorbent* materials. Absorbency is a useful property and is used in various materials, such as kitchen roll and sponges. Sand can be used to soak up potentially dangerous liquids, such as diesel fuel or mercury. Because absorbent materials take in liquid, they increase in weight. Measuring this weight increase, or the reduction in a fixed quantity of a liquid, can help assess absorbency.

Waterproof materials are the opposite of absorbent ones. They are materials that do not soak up liquid but instead resist it. Sometimes this resistance to liquid is natural but sometimes other substances, such as wax, can be added to materials to increase how waterproof they are.

Introduction

- Ask students what they wear, or what they take out with them, when it is raining. Students should explain that they wear coats or carry umbrellas to keep the rain off them. Ask them how they think these items work to keep the rain off them.
- Explain that some materials are waterproof. They do not soak up water, which means they can keep us dry. Ask students to think of three materials that they think are waterproof, and write these on the board underneath the heading 'waterproof'.
- Ask: *What do you do when you spill a liquid?* Students should explain that they wipe the spill up with something.
- Explain that some materials are the opposite of waterproof – they are absorbent. These materials absorb liquids (or soak them up). Ask: *Do you think this is a useful property?* Why? Ask students to think of three absorbent materials, and write them on the board next to the waterproof ones, under the heading 'absorbent'.

Chemistry • Topic 3   Material properties 3.10

Teaching and learning activities

Ask students to look at the pictures on page 64 of their Student's Books. They should work in pairs to discuss the pictures and then answer the questions.

Remind students about soil, which they learned about in Topic 1, and about plants needing water.

Now ask students to look at the pictures on page 65 of their Student's Books. They should discuss the pictures in pairs and then answer the questions. Circulate while they discuss this, making sure they understand the difference between waterproof and absorbent, and that these properties can be useful or harmful depending on the way that they are used.

Ask the class to name any materials that they think are absorbent or waterproof. Write them on the board under the headings 'waterproof' and 'absorbent'. Now ask the class to say what they think would happen if the material was the opposite – for example if a sponge was waterproof instead of absorbent.

More able students could attempt DVD Activity C4 to say which rocks let water in and which keep water out. They will need to use their prior knowledge and some of the ideas they have learned in this topic in order to answer the questions.

Graded activities

As this is a practical investigation, it is recommended that the students work in mixed ability groups for this activity. Differentiation should be through the level of support the students receive as they work on the activity, as well as by outcome (please see guidance in the 'Differentiation' box right).

1 Ask students to name three absorbent and three waterproof materials and explain why it is useful for these materials to be absorbent or waterproof. Ask for examples of objects made from these materials.

2 In groups, students should plan a fair test to discover how waterproof a material or object is. Remind them about the need to make the test fair. Students should draw their experiment on page 55 of their Workbooks.

3 In groups students should first discuss and make predictions for the materials they have chosen. Then students should carry out their test (once you have checked it is safe) and should record their results in the table on page 56 of their Workbooks. Were their predictions correct?

Consolidate and review

- Ask students to think of three more materials to test for absorbency or how waterproof they are. Write the material names on the board and then ask students to predict the results.
- Ask different groups to explain the tests that they used to investigate the materials in Activity 2.
- Ask the class which method they thought was best, and about ways in which they could adapt their own tests to make them fair or more accurate.
- Ask the class why it is useful to know how waterproof or absorbent a material is. Ask: *What would happen if the properties were mixed up?* Students should give an example of these properties switching in both cases.

Differentiation

■ All of the students should be able to name some absorbent and some waterproof materials and explain that waterproof and absorbent are opposites.

● Most of the students should be able to explain why absorbency and being waterproof are useful properties, and should be able to design a fair test to investigate materials for these properties.

▲ Some of the students should be able to explain that these properties can be useful or harmful depending on the way that they are used, and should be able to predict how waterproof or absorbent some materials are. More able students will be able to complete DVD Activity C4 using ideas and information they have learned in this topic.

Chemistry • Topic 3 Material properties 3.11

3.11 Magnets

Student's Book pages 66–67

Chemistry learning objective
- Explore how some materials are magnetic but many are not.

Resources
- Workbook page 57 and 58
- PCM C8: Testing magnets

Classroom equipment
- small steel paperclips
- range of different kinds of magnets: horseshoe, bar, old, new, big, small etc.
- range of magnetic and non-magnetic materials, to include uncoated steel paperclips, plastic coated steel paperclips, aluminium drinks cans, iron nails, plastic objects, wooden objects
- For Activity 3 each group will need a beaker of sand mixed with iron nails or washers, small squares of aluminium cut from drinks cans, safety gloves and eye protection

Scientific enquiry skills
- *Ideas and evidence:* Collect evidence in a variety of contexts to answer questions or test ideas.
- *Plan investigative work:* Suggest ideas, make predictions and communicate these.
- *Obtain and present evidence:* Observe and compare objects, living things and events.
- *Consider evidence and approach:* Draw conclusions from results and begin to use scientific knowledge to suggest explanations; make generalisations and begin to identify simple patterns in results.

Key words
- **magnet**
- **attract**
- **magnetic**

⚠️ Remind students not to drop any of the magnets. They should wear safety gloves and eye protection for Activity 3.

Scientific background

A *magnet* is usually made from a substance that contains iron. A magnet *attracts* other *magnetic* materials. Materials that are attracted to magnets include metals such as iron, some steels, nickel and cobalt. Not all metals are magnetic. Non-magnetic materials include plastic, wood and glass. Magnets attract or repel each other, depending on the orientation of the poles. Similar poles repel but opposite poles attract. The students will learn about forces of attraction in Stage 4 of this course.

Introduction

- Show the students a magnet and a magnetic material. Start with them apart and then move them together. Repeat this several times. Ask: *Why do these stick together?* Explain that one is a magnet and the other is a magnetic material. You should talk about the attraction between certain materials.

- Explain that when you use a magnet you can feel a pulling force when it attracts an object made from a magnetic material.

- Get individual students to come up to your desk and use the magnet to try and pick up objects. As each student has a turn, ask the class: *Is this object magnetic?* When they say yes, or no, develop two separate piles of objects on your desk: those that are magnetic, and those that are not magnetic.

Teaching and learning activities

- Ask the students to look at the pictures on page 66 of the Student's Book. Discuss the objects shown. Ask them to say which objects they think are magnetic and which objects they think are not. If they say that all the metal objects are magnetic, do not correct them at this stage. Encourage students to think of other objects that may be magnetic. Make a list on the board.

Chemistry • Topic 3 Material properties 3.11

- Explain that magnets come in all shapes and sizes. Demonstrate the ones that you have on your desk. Name the shapes – horseshoe, round, bar etc. Tell the students that they are going to investigate some different-shaped magnets to see if the shapes make a difference to the amount of magnetic material they can pick up.
- Get students to work in their groups with different magnets and steel paperclips. Hand out PCM C8 to each group and ask them to complete the activity. They should then do the activities in the Student's Book.

Graded activities

As this is a practical investigation, it is recommended that the students work in mixed ability groups for this activity. Differentiation should be through the level of support the students receive as they work on the activity, as well as by outcome (please see guidance in the 'Differentiation' box bottom right).

1 Give each group a variety of different objects and a magnet to test if they are magnetic or not. Include uncoated metal paperclips, metal paperclips coated in plastic, an aluminium drinks can, a wooden spoon, a metal (steel) spoon, paper, iron nails, coins. They should record their results on page 57 of their Workbook.

2 Provide each student, or group, with a bar magnet. Ask the students to find five magnetic objects in the classroom, and five that are non-magnetic. Ask them to make a list of the magnetic and non-magnetic objects, and the materials they think that each object is made from, on page 58 of their Workbooks.

Once the students have completed Activities 1 and 2, ask them if they can identify a pattern in their results. By now the students should have observed that only certain metal objects are magnetic (iron and steel). The aluminium drinks can from Activity 1 is not magnetic.

Draw attention to the fact that both the uncoated metal paperclips and the plastic coated paperclips were magnetic. Ask: *Does this mean plastic is magnetic?* The students should be able to say that plastic is not magnetic but the magnet is powerful enough to attract the metal through the thin layer of plastic. Make sure that all of the students understand this before moving on to Activity 3, as it will be covered in more detail in the next unit.

3 Let the students discuss in their groups situations when it might be useful to use magnets to separate materials. Lead them to suggest their use when recycling aluminium drinks cans for recycling. The steel cans are picked up by the magnet, leaving the aluminium cans behind. Give each group a beaker of sand mixed with iron nails (or washers) and some small squares of aluminium cut from drinks cans. Let them use a magnet to sort the materials. Please note: the students should wear gloves and eye protection for this investigation. Ask: *How is this investigation similar to sorting aluminium for recycling? Why is it more efficient to use a magnet than to sort the materials by hand?*

Consolidate and review

- Remind students that not all metals are magnetic. They can see that paperclips are indeed magnetic. Show them the way that a magnet picks up some iron nails, but does not pick up a gold ring (or earring), for example. Say that a magnet only attracts objects that are magnetic.
- Get volunteers to test various objects in the classroom. The class members must put up their hands to answer the question asked by the volunteer: *Is this magnetic?*

Differentiation

■ All of the students should be able to recognise that objects which stick (or are attracted) to a magnet are magnetic materials. They will be able to record their results with little or no help.

● Most of the students should be able to state (or guess) that iron and steel are the materials that stick to a magnet. They will begin to recognise that it is the strength of a magnet that enables it to work through other materials.

▲ Some of the students should be able to relate the sorting experiment to the way cans are sorted for recycling. They will be able to complete the investigation safely and suggest reasons why sorting metals using a magnet is better than sorting them by hand.

Chemistry • Topic 3   Material properties 3.12

3.12 Using magnets

Student's Book pages 68–69
Chemistry learning objectives
- Explore how some materials are magnetic but many are not.
- Discuss why materials are chosen for specific purposes on the basis of their properties.

Resources
- Workbook page 59
- Slideshow C4: Uses of magnets

Classroom equipment
- coloured pens or pencils

Scientific enquiry skills
- *Plan investigative work:* Suggest ideas, make predictions and communicate these.
- *Obtain and present evidence:* Observe and compare objects, living things and events.
- *Consider evidence and approach:* Draw conclusions from results and begin to use scientific knowledge to suggest explanations.

Scientific background

Magnets *attract* magnetic objects.

Magnets can be used for making toys, for sorting materials (in aluminum recycling centres, for example), for fridge magnets, and for picking up tools. Magnets are components in motors and generators. Big electromagnets pick up metal cars and parts in scrapyards. Very strong magnets (neodymium magnets) are used in computer hard drives. 50% of all neodymium magnets are found in computer drives.

At Stage 3 the students do not need to know about the poles of a magnet, or about the forces of attraction. The purpose of this unit is to focus on the fact that the size, shape, strength and nature of a magnet depend on what it is to be used for.

Introduction

- As a class, read through the text and questions on Student's Book pages 68-69. Let the students discuss where and how magnets are used in everyday objects at home, and in the classroom.
- Remind the students of their investigation in the previous unit where they discovered that plastic coated paperclips could still be picked up by a magnet. Relate this to the example of the fridge door. If you have a fridge in the science lab or school kitchen, then allow the students to examine how the door opens and closes.

Chemistry • Topic 3　Material properties 3.12

Teaching and learning activities

- Show the students Slideshow C4 which shows some ways that magnets are used in everyday life. Ask if they can think of any other examples.

Graded activities

1 For this activity the students should work individually. They will need to draw upon their knowledge of materials that they have gained in this topic to design a fashionable purse (or handbag) which uses magnets to keep it closed. They should draw a picture of their design on page 59 of their Workbook and label all of the materials used. They should describe what properties of each material make it a suitable choice.

2 In small groups the students should use the internet or books to find out how a magnet in the case of a tablet cover can turn the device on or off. If you are able to show them a tablet with a case that uses a magnet, this will help them to better understand the task. Although this is beyond what is taught at Stage 3, the students should be able to grasp how the magnet is being used even if they do not fully understand the physics involved. This research task will stretch the students and encourage them to think scientifically in order to find a suitable explanation for how it works. The students can give a short presentation to the rest of the class explaining what they have found out.

3 This is a research based activity that more able students will find interesting. They should use the internet or books to find out how computer hard drives (or CD/DVD drives) use magnets. The students will be surprised to learn that there is a powerful magnet inside their computer. The students can work in groups and give a short presentation to the rest of the class explaining what they have found out.

Consolidate and review

- Revise what students know so far about magnets. Write a cloze procedure exercise on the board, and get students to fill in the missing words, or create a magnets wordsearch for them to complete.

Differentiation

■ All of the students should be able to design a purse or handbag. They will need to draw upon their knowledge of material properties when deciding which materials to use. All of the students should be able to explain their choice of materials.

● Most of the students should be able to research how a magnet in a tablet case can turn the device on or off. Less able students may need some additional help with their research.

▲ Some of the students should be able to conduct research with little or no help. They will keep careful notes and be able to present a coherent and scientifically correct presentation to the rest of the class.

Chemistry • Topic 3 Material properties Consolidation

Consolidation

Student's Book page 70
Chemistry learning objectives
- Know that every material has specific properties, e.g. hard, soft, shiny.
- Sort materials according to their properties.
- Explore how some materials are magnetic but many are not.
- Discuss why materials are chosen for specific purposes on the basis of their properties.

Resources
- Assessment Sheets C1, C2 and C3

Looking back

- Use the summary points to review the key knowledge areas students have learned in this topic. Make up some true and false statements based on the summary points. Share these with the class and let the students decide whether the statements are true or false. If they are false, they should correct the statements.

How well do you remember?

You may use the revision and consolidation activities on page 70 either as a test or as a paired class activity. If you are using the activities as a test, have the students work on their own to complete the activities in writing and then collect and mark the work. If you are using them as a class activity, you may prefer to let the students do the tasks orally. Circulate as they discuss the pictures and observe the students to see who is confident, and who is unsure of the concepts.

Some suggested answers
1. They have all been designed to suit their purpose. The materials used have been chosen because of certain properties. Each of them uses steel for strength. The shape of each object helps with its role.
2. Steel – strength / glass – transparency for windows / metal – railing for bridge / metal – radio mast on building, etc.
3. Bridge – triangular struts for strength / boat – lighter material and more air inside (ballast) / building – larger base for more stability.

Assessment

A more formal assessment of the students' understanding of the topic can be undertaken using Assessment Sheets C1, C2 and C3.

Students following Cambridge Assessment International Education Primary Science Curriculum Framework will write progression tests set and supplied by Cambridge at this level and feedback will be given regarding their achievement levels.

Assessment Sheet answers

Sheet C1
1. iron / steel [2]
2. Wooden spoon – hard and rough. Drinks can – round and smooth. Mirror – shiny and flat. T-shirt – soft and flexible. [4]
3. metal / load / wood / strong [4]

Sheet C2
1. weight / shape [2]
2. see-through / strong / waterproof [3]
3. rub [1]
4. true / false / true / false [4]

Sheet C3
1. A hard material...can scratch a soft one. / You can use the dent test...to test the hardness of a material. / Strong materials...do not break easily. [3]
2. a pyramid
   b B
   c Check students' diagram. [3]
3. tick / tick [2]
4. strength / hardness [2]

Chemistry • Topic 3 Material properties Student's Book answers

Student's Book answers

Pages 46–47
1. a The glass block is clear and see-through.
   b It is about the size of a brick.
   c It is hard and smooth.
2. a The straw looks like lots of dry bits of grass all squashed into a brick shape.
   b It is also about the size of the brick.
   c It is bristly and prickly when you touch it.

Pages 48–49
1. Hard materials – stone, metal, wood. Soft materials – plastic, rubber.
2. Check students' answers. Hard materials could be metals; soft materials could be fabrics.
3. The road, because it has to take the weight of lots of cars and trucks. So it will get a lot of use by very heavy objects.
4. You could drop an object onto each surface and see if it dents. To make this fair you would have to drop the same object, from the same height, onto each of the different surfaces.

Pages 50–51
1. His bag was made of a material that was too weak to carry such a heavy load.
2. The third bag. It looks like it is made of strong paper, so it would be able to carry a heavy load of shopping.
3. The hard materials are the glass and the piece of wood. The strong materials are the rope, the plastic bag and the wood. Wood can be both strong and hard.
4. Students could say that rope is useful because it is strong, and can carry heavy weights. A rope that was hard would not be useful as it would be less flexible.

Pages 52–53
1. He is blowing up a balloon.
2. They go back to their original shape.
3. No, some stretchy materials, like clay and dough, stay in the shape you have stretched them to. Others, like rubber bands, go back to their original shape.
4. A life jacket needs to be made of flexible material, so that when you blow it up, it stretches to fill up with air.
5. Very rigid material like canvas would not be suitable for a life jacket, as it would not be flexible enough to inflate.
6. Yes, it is the most suitable material, as it is flexible, and the life jacket can inflate to fill with air when it is blown up.

Page 54–55
1. Wood is used to make furniture, like desks and tables, as well as window frames, door and roof trusses. Metal is used to make bridges, cars, boats and airplanes.
2. Wood is hard, but flexible. It can be carved or cut into different shapes. Metal is hard and inflexible. It is used to build very strong structures.
3. Wood is chosen for objects that need to be shaped easily and be reasonably strong, such as furniture. Metal is chosen for objects that need to be very strong but can be heavier, such as vehicles or buildings.
4. The buildings are all very tall. They are similar shapes. They are different colours and some are bigger than others.
5. The cone-shaped low building in the foreground is more stable than the others, because it has a wider base.
6. Metal and glass have been used to make the buildings. Both materials are strong and inflexible. You can see through glass; that's why it has been used for the windows. The metal is strong enough to hold up very tall buildings.

Pages 56–57
1. Brick, because it is hard and strong but not expensive; also it can look attractive.
2. Glass, because it is see-through and hard.
3. Wood, because it is lighter than metal, can be shaped easily and is hard.
4. Stone, because it is hard but is cheaper and lighter than metal.
5. Glass, because it is see-through but harder than plastic so it doesn't damage easily.

Pages 58–59
1. So they can stretch when we put them on, and do not go out of shape.
2. Because this allows us to wear them many times.
3. Clothes, elastic bands, sling shots etc.
4. Because many sports need balls to bounce, which elastic materials do, and items like tennis rackets use elastic strings to bounce balls back.

Pages 60–61
1. Weight and shape.
2. The amount of air that is trapped in the ship.
3. Big ships usually have air tanks, called ballasts, inside them to help them to float.

Pages 62–63
1. The shop windows, the car windscreen, the people's sunglasses, the glass bottles and drinking glasses.
2. No, some glass is cloudy (it lets in light, but you can't see through it) and some glass is not see-through (it doesn't let in any light and you can't see through it).
3. Glasses, bottles, light bulbs, cell phone displays, camera lenses.
4. Check students' answers. Possible answers include vases, front doors, decorative items.

Pages 64–65
1. Because plants need water to grow, and absorbent soil will hold more water, so it will be good for planting.
2. Paper, sponge, sand and fabric.
3. Wood, stone and glass.
4. Check students' answers.
5. To keep us dry in rainy weather, to keep water out of our houses, to keep water off us in rainy weather.
6. We would get wet; our houses would flood from the ceilings; we would get wet.

Pages 66–67
1. no
2. Steel paperclip, steel ruler, steel nail. You could use a magnet to see if it sticks to the object.
3. It attracts all of the steel cans and leaves the aluminium ones behind.
4. Aluminium is lightweight and easily recycled. Steel is stronger and harder to crush so it is good for protecting food.

Pages 68–69
1. Students' own answers.
2. The magnet is attracted to the metal door frame and when they stick together they seal the door shut.
3. To fit in the fridge door the magnet has to be the right shape: thin, long and flexible.

Physics • Topic 4 Forces and motion

4.1 Pushes and pulls

Student's Book pages 72–73

Physics learning objective
- Know that pushes and pulls are examples of forces and that they can be measured with forcemeters.

Resources
- Workbook pages 60 and 61
- DVD Activity P1: Forces and movement

Classroom equipment
- bar magnets
- wooden blocks
- selection of toys and household items that work by being pushed or pulled, including some magnetic examples
- colouring pens or pencils

Scientific enquiry skills
- *Ideas and evidence:* Collect evidence in a variety of contexts to answer questions or test ideas.
- *Plan investigative work:* Suggest ideas, make predictions and communicate these.

Key words
- **push**
- **pull**

Scientific background

Pushes and *pulls* are forces; you can use these as simple definitions of a force, i.e. a force is a push or a pull.

Forces cannot be seen but they can be felt. The students will need the opportunity to try out pushing and pulling for themselves. The effects of forces can be seen in the resulting motion. Strength and direction of forces can be changed and will result in changed motion. The students will need to see what happens to toys when they are pushed and pulled.

Introduction

- Place a simple block on the table in front of each pair. Ask the students if the block is moving. Now ask the students to use their hands to make the block move. Ask: *How did you do this?* Then ask the students to move the block again, this time in the opposite direction.
- Encourage the students to use the words *push* and *pull* to describe their actions. Explain that pushes and pulls are types of *forces*.
- Introduce the idea of direction, although students don't need to know the term yet. Ask: *Which way were you moving the block?* Say: *So, the force was moving away from you/towards you/sideways.* Ask the students to explain each other's actions. For example, he pushed the block away from him; she pulled the block towards her.
- Now experiment with magnets. This is revision work, as the students have already covered magnets in Topic 3. Demonstrate with two bar magnets. Ask: *How can I make the two magnets push away from each other? What do I need to change to make the two magnets pull towards each other?* Make sure that students understand these are push and pull forces.

Teaching and learning activities

- Get the students to look at the toys in the pictures on page 72 of the Student's Book. In pairs, they should decide which of the toys need to be pushed to make them move and which need to be pulled. Students should discuss and decide on the answers for the rest of the questions. Take feedback from the class to make sure everyone has understood the concepts of force, push and pull.

Physics • Topic 4   Forces and motion 4.1

- Talk about examples of pushes and pulls in everyday life and refer to the pictures on page 73. What other examples can the students think of? Talk through the questions as a class.
- Ask the students to think about push and pull forces that are used in sport. Let them give some examples. Sports they might suggest include archery (pull), skiing (push), kicking a football (push). If any students are still struggling with the concept of push and pull, say that a push is an action away from your body and a pull is an action towards your body. Demonstrate this as necessary.

Graded activities

1 The students should sort another group of objects into those involving pushing or pulling forces. You can include everyday household items, for example a tin opener, a grater, a light switch, a flashlight, a broom, etc. Students divide the objects into the two groups and write the lists in their exercise books under the headings 'push' and 'pull'.

2 The students should work individually to complete the activity on page 60 of their Workbook. They should circle push forces in red and pull forces in blue. They should also write a sentence describing the way one of their toys works in terms of pushes and pulls, for example a computer game may require a joystick to be pushed and pulled.

3 Students should think about all the push and pull forces they experience on a normal school day. For example, opening doors, pulling on shoes, etc. They should make a list and record their observations in their Workbooks on page 61.

Consolidate and review

- Talk about pushes and pulls in the classroom. What force do you use to open your desk, or to open the window or door?
- Discuss other pushes and pulls that students can think of. For example, ask: *How does the gardener move the lawnmower? How do you get a car with a flat battery to move? How do you get your jersey over your head?* Encourage the students to be alert to the pushes and pulls around them, and to become aware of how much is moving around them and what is making it move.
- Let the students complete DVD Activity P1 to recap what they have learned in Stage 1 and to consolidate the learning from this unit.

Differentiation

■ All of the students should be able to correctly sort a group of objects into those that work by pushing and those that work by pulling.

● Most of the students should be able to complete the activity with little or no help. They should be able to write a short sentence about one of their toys. Less able students may require additional help using the correct vocabulary.

▲ Some of the students should be able to compile a comprehensive list of all the push and pull forces they have experienced that day.

Physics • Topic 4 Forces and motion 4.2

4.2 Making things move

Student's Book pages 74–75
Physics learning objective
- Explore how forces can make objects start or stop moving.

Resources
- Workbook pages 62 and 63
- PCM P1: Push, pull, twist

Classroom equipment
- bottle with screw top
- toys or household items that move with a push, pull or twist
- identical toy cars or balls
- chalk
- coloured pens or pencils

Scientific enquiry skills
- *Ideas and evidence:* Collect evidence in a variety of contexts to answer questions or test ideas.
- *Plan investigative work:* Suggest ideas, make predictions and communicate these; with help, think about collecting evidence and planning fair tests.
- *Consider evidence and approach:* Make generalisations and begin to identify simple patterns in results.

Key words
- stationary
- twist

Scientific background

Forces affect objects in different ways. This unit focuses on the idea that a force can make an object start to move. Without friction or air resistance, an object would keep moving at the same speed, without the need for any extra force. However, in everyday conditions friction and air resistance act to slow down moving objects. This is why in science we talk about a force being needed to make an object start to move. Students should be able to observe that objects remain *stationary* unless a force acts upon them.

Introduction

- Ask three volunteer students to come up to the front of the class. Ask one to demonstrate a push, another to demonstrate a pull, and the last one to show you how something moves by *twisting*. You could put a water bottle with a screw top on the table at that moment to give them a clue.
- Ask the class if they can think of any other examples of where a force is a twist. If you have no responses, turn the doorknob to open the door. Ask: *What kind of force am I applying?* Mime putting your car keys into the ignition and turning the key. Ask: *What kind of force am I applying now?*
- Ask students to say what the bottle top was doing before the student twisted it. Students should say that it was not doing anything. Make sure that they understand that a force is needed to move an object.

Teaching and learning activities

- Ask the students to look at the pictures of the toys on page 74 of the Student's Book. Discuss what each toy is and ask students to name the kind of force it needs to move.
- Ask the students to do the activity on page 62 of the Workbook. In each circle they should draw a toy that matches the kind of force written down. If you feel that drawing toys is too 'young' for your students, you can invite them to draw or write the name of any object that moves by pushing, pulling or twisting.
- Now study the children on page 75 of the Student's Book as a class. Ask a student to describe what the children are doing. Explain that if you apply a force, it makes something move. Demonstrate by sweeping something off your desk, like a pencil.

Physics • Topic 4 Forces and motion 4.2

- Get a volunteer to explain how they would set up the race track in the picture. *How many lanes do you need? How long should they be? How many cars do you need?* Now ask: *If you were testing how much force would move a toy car, how would you make this a fair test? What would you have to keep the same? What would you change?*

Graded activities

As Activities 2 and 3 form part of a practical investigation, it is recommended that the students work in mixed ability groups for these activities. Differentiation should be through the level of support the students receive as they work on the activity, as well as by outcome (please see guidance in the 'Differentiation' right).

1 The students should complete the activity on page 62 of their Workbook. They should draw an object in each circle that matches the kind of force written down and then answer the questions. Less able students may need some prompting to answer question 3. Suggest that a paper boat or a windmill can be made to move if you blow at them. This is a pushing force.

2 In groups, let the students experiment with car races. This is best done in the school grounds or in a cleared area of the classroom. A level surface is best if possible. Ask each group to mark out the tracks with chalk. Circulate, making sure the lengths are equal and the lines are straight. If you don't have cars, you can use tennis balls, or any set of balls that are the same size.

Have a few practice rounds before you do the 'real' race. Say: *On your marks, get set, go!* On this signal, the groups must push the cars or roll the balls. You may have to remind students that you are testing the size of the force, so one person should push only lightly, another with more force, and the last one pushes very strongly.

Students should now return to class or their desks and record the results of their test in their Workbooks on page 63. Substitute 'ball' for 'car', if you have had to adapt the test.

3 Run the same test as with the cars, but by rolling balls instead. This reinforces the test you did with the cars.

Consolidate and review

- Ask students questions about the amount of force needed to do certain things. Provide them with certain examples: for example, push a car, open a bottle, pull a loaded wagon, push a wheelbarrow full of straw. Now let them rate the amount of force needed on a scale of 1 to 5, with 1 being the smallest force and 5 the biggest.

- Hold up the toys and household objects one by one. As you hold them up, the class must call out the kind of force needed to move it. If you would prefer to do this more quietly, tell each student to write 'push', 'pull' and 'twist' on pieces of paper and to hold up the correct piece of paper each time you produce an item.

- Hand out copies of PCM P1 for the students to carry out a 'matching' activity.

Differentiation

■ All of the students should be able to draw three objects that respectively use a push, a pull and a twist. Less able students may require additional help with question.

● ▲ Most of the students should understand that a force needs to be applied to make something move and be able to demonstrate this in a test involving toy cars or balls. Some of the students should be able to explain how to make a fair test showing that a force needs to be applied to make an object move. Most of the students should be able to record their results and conclude that the greater the force applied, the further the car/ball moved.

Physics • Topic 4 Forces and motion 4.3

4.3 Natural forces

Student's Book pages 76–77
Physics learning objective
- Explore how forces can make objects stop or start moving.

Resources
- Workbook pages 64 and 65
- Video P1: Falling water
- Video P2: Wind turbines and waterwheels

Classroom equipment
- straws
- a shallow tray of water for each group
- paper or foil for making boats
- pieces of firm card to make waves
- a non-fragile object to drop

Scientific enquiry skills
- *Ideas and evidence:* Collect evidence in a variety of contexts to answer questions or test ideas.
- *Plan investigative work:* Suggest ideas, make predictions and communicate these; with help, think about collecting evidence and planning fair tests.
- *Consider evidence and approach:* Draw conclusions from results and begin to use scientific knowledge to suggest explanations.

⚠ Ensure that the students take care with water, and that adults help with this equipment. Mop up any water spillages immediately to avoid slipping.

Scientific background

Wind can provide a pushing force on an object. The stronger the wind, the greater the pushing force. At this age the students have not been taught about gases. They may think that air is 'nothing'. It is important that the students feel the force of moving air for themselves so that they can understand this unit.

On a ship, a larger sail means that the force of the wind acts over a larger area. This provides a greater force overall.

Water can push with a large force. Damage caused by flowing water during flooding is evidence of this.

The waterwheel and windmill are examples of humans using the pushing force of water and wind to do a job. Doing these jobs by hand would take a lot more energy, so these are more efficient machines that harness natural forces.

Introduction

- Ask the students to copy your actions. Hold up a hand in front of your face and blow gently into your hand. As the students blow into their hands, ask: *What do you feel?*
- Then hold a piece of paper in front of your face and ask the students to copy you again. Blow on the paper. As they blow on the paper, ask: *What happens when you blow on the paper?*

- Now direct the students to look at the pictures on page 76 of their Student's Books. Ask them what is making the sailing boat, the dinghy and the sand yacht in the pictures move. If you get the answer 'wind' ask them to use more scientific language and try to elicit the response, 'the force of the wind is pushing the sails'.
- Now turn to page 77 and ask the students what other natural force they can see in the picture. The answer is wind, but again, try to encourage students to say, 'the force of the wind is moving the windmill'.
- Discuss wind and water as natural forces. Get students to share stories of how these two forces may have affected their lives. Has anyone been in a flood? Has anyone had things break in a strong wind? Be sensitive to students' personal experiences, which may have been traumatic.

Teaching and learning activities

- Let the students discuss the pictures of boats on page 76 and answer the questions in pairs. Circulate while they are doing this and assist where necessary.

Physics • Topic 4 Forces and motion 4.3

- Show the class Video P1 of a powerful natural waterfall and a human-made hydro-electric power station. Discuss the fact that the falling water produces a very large force. Tell the students that, in countries with a lot of water, the force of falling water can be used to turn machines to generate electric power, this is known as 'hydro-electric' power. The students do not need to know about hydro-electric power as part of the Cambridge Primary Science curriculum, it is included here as enrichment and for additional information only.

- Look at the windmill in the Student's Book. Ask: *What makes the windmill turn?* Explain that windmills were once built to use the force of wind to do useful jobs. In some countries they were used to grind flour. Ask: *How do you think a windmill helps people?* Students should see that it saves human effort by using a natural force.

Graded activities

As Activities 1 and 2 form part of a practical investigation, it is recommended that the students work in mixed ability groups for these activities. Differentiation should be through the level of support the students receive as they work on the activity, as well as by outcome (please see guidance in the 'Differentiation' box right).

1 Students first experiment with the power of water. Set up their trays with a little water in and give them paper or foil to make sailboats. They should remember the way to make a boat from the previous topic, but guide them if they cannot remember.

Hand out pieces of card and tell students that they can use it to make waves. Ask them to experiment by making weaker and stronger waves – weak, medium and strong – and measuring how far the boat moves. Explain that it is hard to make this test fair, but they should record their observations on page 64 of their Workbooks.

2 Now ask students to keep their boats and water trays, but this time use straws to blow against the boat. Ask them to blow softly, a little more, and a lot, and to record their observations in their Workbooks on page 65.

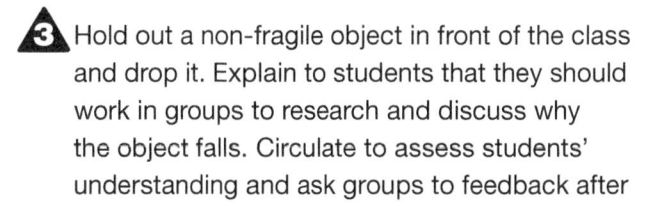

3 Hold out a non-fragile object in front of the class and drop it. Explain to students that they should work in groups to research and discuss why the object falls. Circulate to assess students' understanding and ask groups to feedback after their research.

This Activity will give the students an introduction to the idea of gravity. Gravity will be covered in the next unit.

Consolidate and review

- Show the class Video P2 of wind turbines and waterwheels in action to reinforce the idea that wind and water power can produce a lot of force.

- Discuss waterwheels. Encourage the students to make comments and suggestions for how the waterwheel works and ways in which it could be improved.

- Students should answer the questions on page 77 of the Student's Book in their pairs.

Differentiation

■ All of the students should be able to set up the experiment and make some paper boats. They should be able to follow the instructions in the Workbook, with some help. More able students will be able to say why this is not a fair test (the students may not all use the same amount of force to make the waves).

● Most of the students should be able to record their experiments with wind accurately in their Workbooks, with some help, and understand why boats have sails.

▲ Some of the students should be able to independently research why objects always fall towards the ground (Earth). They will feedback their research to the class in a coherent and organised way.

Big Cat

Students who have read *Big Cat The wind* may recall the different ways in which the power of the wind can be used by humans. The wind can help with leisure activities, from flying a kite to sailing a boat. It can also power windmills, which were originally used to grind cereals such as flour, and are now connected to generators to produce electric power.

Physics • Topic 4 Forces and motion 4.4

4.4 Measuring forces

Student's Book pages 78–79
Physics learning objective
- Know that pushes and pulls are examples of forces and that they can be measured with forcemeters.

Resources
- Workbook pages 66 and 67
- Video P3: Uses of springs
- PCM P2: Springs and masses

Classroom equipment
- non-fragile objects to drop
- newton meters
- springs
- hooked mass hangers
- slotted masses
- clamps and stands, or other means of suspending springs
- strips of paper 1 cm wide
- selection of objects for the students to weigh

Scientific enquiry skills
- *Ideas and evidence:* Collect evidence in a variety of contexts to answer questions or test ideas.
- *Plan investigative work:* Suggest ideas, make predictions and communicate these.
- *Obtain and present evidence:* Measure using simple equipment and record observations in a variety of ways.
- *Consider evidence and approach:* Draw conclusions from results and begin to use scientific knowledge to suggest explanations.

Key words
- **gravity**
- **force meter**
- **newton meter**
- **newtons**
- **weight**

⚠ The students must take care when letting go of stretched materials. They must not stretch the springs too far in case they break.

Scientific background

Springs stretch or compress in a controlled way as more force is added. This means that they can be used in force-measuring equipment, such as *newton meters* (Newton meters are also called *force meters* or spring balances.)

Springs are used in many everyday measuring devices, including those used to weigh ingredients for cooking. They are also sometimes used to weigh suitcases at an airport.

If too much force is applied, a spring can break. It is important that the students understand this so that they don't damage the springs they are using in the investigation.

It is important to realise that there is a difference between an object's *mass* (measured in *grams* or *kilograms*) and its *weight* (measured in *newtons*). At Stage 3 the terms are effectively interchangeable, but you should try to use the term *weight* when describing a force and *mass* otherwise. Strictly, an object's weight is the force exerted by gravity on its *mass*.

All objects are pulled towards the centre of the Earth by *gravity*. The force on an object due to gravity is called its *weight*. This is measured, like other forces, in *newtons*. Everyday scales convert newtons into grams, kilograms etc. but these are actually units for *mass*. On the Moon the pull of gravity is much less. If you used a newton meter on the Moon the weight of objects would be much less than their weight on Earth. However, their *mass* would not change. The objects are still made of the same amount of material.

Introduction

- You will probably find your students have an instinctive understanding of gravity. Drop a non-fragile object on the floor. Ask: *Why did that fall down and not float up?* Demonstrate with another object, asking the same question. Explain that gravity is a force that acts on everything on Earth, pulling things downward.

Physics • Topic 4 Forces and motion 4.4

- Ask: *How would you measure gravity?* This is a complex question. Accept answers like 'you measure how much it pulls down', or 'how much it pulls to the ground'. Introduce the term 'weight' and say your weight is how much of you there is pulling down to the ground.
- Show the class Video P3 on uses of springs. Discuss why springs are necessary for certain jobs. Demonstrate, with a spring, how it can be stretched and compressed.
- Hook a spring onto a hooked mass hanger and pull down on it. Ask: *Could we use this to measure weight?*

Teaching and learning activities

- Direct the students to page 78 of the Student's Book. Look at the pictures and discuss in more detail how a spring can be used to measure forces. Demonstrate how to use a newton meter.
- Let the students discuss the questions in the Student's Book on pages 78 and 79 in their groups. While they are talking about the pictures and answering the questions, walk around the class and give each group a Newton meter and some weights for the graded activities, which follow.

Graded activities

1 In groups and using PCM P2, the students should investigate the way in which the length of a spring changes when you add more masses to it.

2 In groups, the students use newton meters to weigh a selection of objects carefully and record their results in their Workbooks on page 66.

3 Ask students to use their imagination to imagine what life would be like without gravity. They should write two paragraphs or act out a short play to the rest of the class.

Consolidate and review

- Take feedback about the experiments. What was difficult to do? What was easy? Who had the heaviest/lightest weight?
- Ask the class to share some of their writing about gravity. Get volunteers to stand up and read out their stories.
- The students complete the activity on page 67 of their Workbooks to consolidate what they have learned.

Differentiation

■ All of the students should understand that gravity is a downward force that acts on everything on Earth.

● Most of the students should understand that the downward pull of gravity is called weight and that we can measure weight.

▲ Some of the students will be able to measure the force of gravity using a newton meter and will be able to suggest what life would be like without gravity.

Physics • Topic 4 Forces and motion 4.5

4.5 Stopping and starting

Student's Book pages 80–81

Physics learning objective
- Explore how forces can make objects start or stop moving.

Resources
- Workbook pages 68 and 69

Classroom equipment
- balls of different sizes
- measuring tape
- coloured pens or pencils
- large sheets of paper or card (optional)

Scientific enquiry skills
- *Ideas and evidence:* Collect evidence in a variety of contexts to answer questions or test ideas.
- *Plan investigative work:* Suggest ideas, make predictions and communicate these; with help, think about collecting evidence and planning fair tests.
- *Obtain and present evidence:* Observe and compare objects, living things and events; present results in drawings, bar charts and tables.
- *Consider evidence and approach:* Make generalisations and begin to identify simple patterns in results.

Key word
- direction

> ⚠ Make sure the playground activity is supervised.

Scientific background

The speed of an object depends on the force exerted on it. For example, the faster or harder something is thrown, the greater the speed at which it travels.

The mass of an object is also a factor. A larger force is needed to start a heavier object or to stop a faster-moving object.

Note that students will often confuse the *size* of an object and the *mass* of an object.

Introduction

- Have a selection of different sized balls for the students to look at. You may want to conduct this lesson in the school grounds.
- Ask: *Imagine you are catching a ball. What does it feel like when the ball hits your hands?* Throw a tennis ball or bean bag to a volunteer. Then throw the ball or bean bag faster and discuss with the volunteer what force they feel. Ask: *Is it different?*
- The students should observe that they feel a greater force when the ball is thrown faster and when the ball is heavier. If the students comment on the size of the ball, encourage them to consider how heavy each ball is.

Physics • Topic 4 Forces and motion 4.5

Teaching and learning activities

- Next, ask the students to look at the pictures of the goalkeeper on page 80 of the Student's Book. Ask: *Why is the goalkeeper falling over in the second picture?* (Faster ball, larger force)
- Ask the students to discuss the questions in their pairs. Circulate and assist where necessary.
- Next ask the students to think about cars moving on a road. Ask: *What happens if a fast-moving vehicle hits another object?* (It will crash with a large force.) Remind the students that cars are large, fast-moving objects and that they should be very careful when crossing the road.

Graded activities

1 In the school grounds, the students work in pairs throwing balls back and forth, experimenting with different degrees of force. Warn students that they must try not to hurt each other.

2 Now ask the pairs to investigate rolling different-sized balls. One student rolls a ball towards another student, then the other student measures how far the ball travels before it comes to rest. They should try this with at least three different-sized balls. Circulate to make sure that this is a fair test. Ask each group: *What is the variable? What other things must all be kept the same?* Back in the classroom, the students should complete the results graph in their Workbooks on page 68.

3 Students should make a road safety poster for younger children. They can draw the poster on page 69 of their Workbooks, or make a larger poster on a sheet of card.

Consolidate and review

- Sum up by saying that a large force requires a large effort to stop it, and a small force needs only a small effort to stop it.
- Discuss the results of the ball rolling and stopping investigation. Ask: *What were the challenges? Was it difficult to make this a fair test?*
- Collect the Workbooks so you can assess the results of the investigations, and check that the bar chart is correctly filled in. You can also assess the Road Safety poster on a 5-star rating system.

Differentiation

■ All of the students should understand that an object moved by a bigger force requires more effort to stop it than one moved by a smaller force.

● Most of the students should be able to demonstrate that an object moved by a bigger force requires more effort to stop it than one moved by a smaller force through their investigations into rolling and stopping balls. They should be able to record the results of this investigation accurately on a bar chart.

▲ Some of the students will be able to apply their knowledge of forces and understand that a fast-moving car is harder to stop than a slow-moving car. They should be able to produce a road safety poster for young children that delivers this message.

Physics • Topic 4 Forces and motion 4.6

4.6 Changing direction

Student's Book pages 82–83

Physics learning objective
- Explore how forces, including friction, can make objects move faster or slower or change direction.

Resources
- Workbook pages 70 and 71
- Video P4: Footballers
- Video P5: Ice hockey

Classroom equipment
- marbles
- students' own toy cars/vehicles
- chalk to mark the test area

Scientific enquiry skills
- *Ideas and evidence:* Collect evidence in a variety of contexts to answer questions or test ideas.
- *Plan investigative work:* Suggest ideas, make predictions and communicate these.
- *Obtain and present evidence:* Observe and compare objects, living things and events.
- *Consider evidence and approach:* Make generalisations and begin to identify simple patterns in results.

Key word
- applying

⚠️ Make sure the playground activity is supervised. Ensure that students behave sensibly with the marbles and toys as these are possible tripping risks. The marbles and toy cars should stay on the table/floor, and not be hit into the air.

Scientific background

Forces can make an object start to move, they can stop an object and they can also change the direction of an object.

This is very important in physics and is why the Moon orbits the Earth. The pull of gravity changes the Moon's direction and stops it from travelling in a straight line out into space. The students will understand the concept better with everyday examples, for example, a footballer changing the direction of the ball to shoot at a goal or two snooker balls hitting each other.

Introduction

- Review Activities 2 and 3 from the last lesson. Give feedback to the groups about their bar charts. Ask the class to vote on the best road safety poster.
- Tell the students they are now going to study the ways that forces can change the direction of moving objects. Show Video P4 of footballers. Ask: *What force are the footballers using? What is that force doing?* (Although the students may recall this video from Stage 1, the focus at Stage 3 is on how a force can make an object change direction.)
- Introduce the idea that a force can change the direction of a moving object.
- Show the students Video P5 of an ice-hockey game. Tell them to watch the direction changes of the ice puck carefully. They should note that the force of the hockey stick frequently changes the direction of the moving puck.

Teaching and learning activities

- Ask the students to look at page 82 of the Student's Book and answer the questions. They should discuss their answers in small groups.
- The pictures show three ways that a force can affect the movement of an object. Picture 2 shows the ball starting to move. Force is being applied to a stationary object. Picture 1 shows the ball changing direction because it comes in from one direction and is 'headed' in another direction. (This is because the force has changed the direction of the movement.) Picture 3 shows a force being applied to a moving ball and stopping it.

Physics • Topic 4   Forces and motion 4.6

Graded activities

1 Ask the students to work in their pairs to complete the activity on page 70 of their Workbooks. This investigation can be done outside if necessary.

2 Students now plan their own investigation to see what happens when a force changes the direction of a moving object. They should do this in the school grounds, as it is quite noisy. Each pair should bring their own toy cars/vehicles to school for this investigation. The pairs should now write down what they did and what they observed and draw a diagram of their investigation in their Workbooks on page 71.

3 The students should copy or trace the pictures from Student's Book page 83 onto a sheet of blank paper. Using their knowledge of forces they should then draw on arrows to show the direction of the object at the start, and the change of direction.

Consolidate and review

● Take feedback from the different pairs. Who had a particularly good result? What kind of cars worked best? How difficult was it to aim them in the right direction, to ensure that they crashed?

● Discuss what the students have learned about forces so far. Make a mind map on the board as you manage the discussion, adding the information about forces that the class provide.

Differentiation

■ All of the students should be able to see that a moving object, when hit by a force, will change direction. They should be able to point out the picture in which this happens in their books. They will be able to complete the activity with some help. Less able students will need help writing the conclusion. (A force can change the direction of an object.)

● Most of the students should be able to demonstrate practically the way that a force can make an object change direction. They will be able to plan their own investigation using toys or other suitable objects.

▲ Some of the students will be able to accurately draw on arrows to show the direction of the object at the start, and the change of direction. More able students may begin to relate the length of the arrow to the amount of force applied or exerted.

Physics • Topic 4 Forces and motion 4.7

4.7 Changing shape

Student's Book pages 84–85

Physics learning objective
- Explore how forces can change the shape of objects.

Resources
- Workbook pages 72, 73 and 74
- Video P6: Shaping metal

Classroom equipment
- dough (optional)
- modelling clay
- coloured pens or pencils

Scientific enquiry skills
- *Ideas and evidence:* Collect evidence in a variety of contexts to answer questions or test ideas.
- *Obtain and present evidence:* Measure using simple equipment and record observations in a variety of ways.

Key words
- **squeeze**
- **dent**
- **bend**

Scientific background

Forces can change the shape of some materials. Materials can be pushed together (*squashed* and *squeezed*) or pulled apart (*stretched*).

The students will be familiar with the term 'elastic' from their knowledge of material properties. They know that an elastic material is one that returns to its original shape after a stretching force is removed.

The focus here is on the force being *applied*. When the force is pulling on an elastic object it will stretch. When the force is removed it returns to its starting shape. Non-elastic materials either do not stretch when pulled or do not return to their starting shape when the pulling force is removed.

This unit extends the students' vocabulary to include words for changing the shape of non-elastic materials. These include *bend* and *dent*. These words apply to materials that are flexible or malleable (can be changed in shape by hammering or other similar processes).

Introduction

- If you are able to get a baker or a potter to come and demonstrate how they handle their materials, that would be a very good introduction to this unit. The person can demonstrate different forces – pushing, pulling, stretching, squashing and denting. If you are able to make dough and bring it to class, you can be the 'Visiting Baker'. Alternatively, you can set the students a task to investigate either pottery or baking with the aim of explaining these forces.

- Ask students to look at the pictures on page 84 of the Student's Book. Ask: *What forces can you see at work here?* Make sure the students understand that it is the force of the baker's hands that is changing the shape of the dough, a collision with another object that caused the dent, and the squeezing force on the rubber ball that has squashed it.

Physics • Topic 4 Forces and motion 4.7

Teaching and learning activities

- The students should work in groups to study the pictures on pages 84 and 85 of their Student's Books and answer the questions.
- The students should then do the activity in their Workbooks on page 72. Here they have to identify which kind of force is being used in each picture. This revises the work students have covered so far.

Graded activities

1 Each student should have a chance to work with a lump of clay, to experiment with the different forces which can be applied to it, and to look at the resulting shapes. Take feedback as the activity is in progress and encourage students by pointing out good examples of student work, such as squashing, rolling etc.

The students should then wash their hands and return to their desks. They should draw their clay before and after the investigation and then write a short description of what they did, using correct scientific terms. They can complete this on page 73 of their Workbooks.

2 In their groups students discuss forces and the ways that they can change the shapes of objects. They should draw up a group mind map showing all they have learned about forces so far. Make sure you have erased your diagram from the previous lesson from the board so that students do not copy it.

3 Ask students to research the ways that forces can be used to shape metal. They can look at car manufacturing, panel beaters etc. Use Video P6 to open the activity and then ask students to fill in the table on page 74 of their Workbooks.

Consolidate and review

- Have a quick quiz. Call out these words and ask the students to give you an example of each of them: *push*, *pull*, *stretch*, *squash*, *dent* and *squeeze*.
- Discuss the mind maps the groups drew up. What is similar in all of them? What is different? Did any group have a particularly interesting branch on their mind map? You could ask the groups to each come up and write one point on the board, so that you develop a class mind map.

Differentiation

■ All of the students should be able to work with clay and experiment with applying different kinds of forces to the clay. Most of the students should be able to name these forces, and say where the forces are coming from. Some of the students should be able to use scientific terms like 'direction', 'apply', 'weight' etc. in their description of the forces acting on the clay and dough.

● Most of the students should be able to discuss what they know about forces and produce a mind map. They should all contribute towards the activity although more able students may tend to lead the activity.

▲ Some of the students should be able to undertake independent research. They will complete the questions in their Workbook with little or no help.

Physics • Topic 4 Forces and motion 4.8

4.8 Friction

Student's Book pages 86–87

Physics learning objective
- Explore how forces, including friction, can make objects move faster or slower or change direction.

Resources
- Workbook pages 75 and 76
- PCM P3: Bicycle brakes

Classroom equipment
- heavy object to push across the table to show friction, e.g. a large box
- selection of balls
- coloured pens or pencils

Scientific enquiry skills
- *Ideas and evidence:* Collect evidence in a variety of contexts to answer questions or test ideas.
- *Plan investigative work:* Suggest ideas, make predictions and communicate these.
- *Obtain and present evidence:* Present results in drawings, bar charts and tables.
- *Consider evidence and approach:* Draw conclusions from results and begin to use scientific knowledge to suggest explanations.

Key word
- friction

Scientific background

When a moving object or surface is in contact with another surface, a force called *friction* opposes the movement. Friction acts in the opposite direction to the motion. An ice-skater moves easily because there is little friction between the ice and the blades of the skates. A mountaineer moving on rough ground will experience more friction between his boots and the ground. A bike travelling over tarmac will experience friction on its wheels.

Friction is very useful as it makes it possible for us to walk. Without friction we would slip along. Friction between car tyres and the road helps the car to stay on the road. Friction between brake pads and wheels means we can stop bicycles or cars quickly.

Sometimes friction can be wasteful. The rubbing between two surfaces often causes heat, and continual rubbing can wear out the materials the surfaces are made from. Oil is often used as a lubricant between two surfaces that rub together, to reduce friction and stop them from squeaking or wearing out.

Introduction

- Walk across the front of the classroom. Ask: *What force is moving me forward?* The students will say you are moving yourself forward. Ask: *Is there anything slowing me down?* Then ask: *If I were skating on an ice rink, would I be moving slower or faster?* Point out to the students that the ground provides friction, which slows you down. If there was no friction, you would glide forwards much faster.

- Give each group a ball to roll, and practise rolling the ball across different surfaces. Try the classroom floor, a smooth surface like a table top, and a rough surface like a gravel path, perhaps in the school grounds.

- Explain to the class that friction is a force that acts in the opposite direction to the movement. Draw an example on the board, with arrows. Demonstrate that pushing a box across the table makes a grating sound. Tell students that the noise is a result of friction. Draw the box on the board and then draw arrows to show the direction of movement (your push) and the direction of friction (opposite).

Physics • Topic 4 Forces and motion 4.8

Teaching and learning activities

- Talk about the drawings on page 86. Can the students see the direction of movement? And the direction of friction? Ask for volunteers to explain the term 'friction'. Answers that use the words 'rubbing' or 'squeaking' are good.

- Get volunteers to talk about where there is friction in their surroundings. Does the desk or door hinge squeak? That is because two surfaces are rubbing against each other.

- Explain that friction can also be very useful. Ask the students to look at the pictures on the page 87 of their Student's Book. Can they see that there is friction operating in each example? Let them discuss this in pairs, quietly.

Graded activities

1 The students should copy or trace the pictures from page 87 of the Student's Book into their exercise books and draw arrows to show the directions of the friction and the movement. They can then follow this by doing the activity in their Workbooks on page 75, where they use coloured pencils to show the movement and the friction, and complete a paragraph by filling in the missing words.

2 The students work individually to write a paragraph about where friction helps or hinders their daily transport. Look out for positive points like brakes, handlebar grips, tread on shoes or tyres, and negative points like the heat caused by friction, or squeaky noises. They can draw two examples of this in their Workbooks on page 76, or in their exercise books.

3 Set the students a research task about a place where friction is useful. If this seems too ambitious, let them complete PCM P3 about bicycle brakes unaided.

Consolidate and review

- Take feedback about ways in which friction helps or hinders the students in their transport to and from school every day. Let the students express their frustration with the squeaky brakes on the school bus, or the way their bike brakes get very hot after the ride home and wear out in time.

Differentiation

■ All of the students should be able to identify, with arrows, the direction of the movement and the direction of friction.

● Most of the students should be able to describe ways in which friction can be useful or a hindrance, and give examples of each. They will be able to draw two example in their Workbook with little or no help.

▲ Some of the students should be able to undertake research unaided. Less able students may require some additional help.

Physics • Topic 4 Forces and motion Consolidation

Consolidation

Student's Book page 88
Physics learning objectives
- Know that pushes and pulls are examples of forces and that they can be measured with forcemeters.
- Explore how forces can make objects start or stop moving.
- Explore how forces can change the shape of objects.
- Explore how forces, including friction, can make objects move faster or slower or change direction.

Resources
- Assessment Sheets P1, P2 and P3

Looking back
- Use the summary points to review the key knowledge areas students have learned in this topic. Make up some true and false statements based on the summary points. Share these with the class and let the students decide whether the statements are true or false. If they are false, they should correct the statements.
- Ask students to write down three sentences about things they have learned in this topic. Let them tell the group why they found these things interesting.

How well do you remember?

You may use the revision and consolidation activities on page 88 of the Student's Book either as a test or as a paired class activity. If you are using the activities as a test, have the students work on their own to complete the activities in writing and then collect and mark the work. If you are using them as a class activity, you may prefer to let the students do the tasks orally. Circulate as they discuss the pictures and observe the students to see who is confident and who is unsure of the concepts.

Some suggested answers
1. pull / forwards/ the plough moves
2. push / towards the toy / the turn turns
3. push / forwards / the ship moves
4. pull / downwards / the string stretches
5. push / against the direction the ball is moving / the ball stops
6. push / in the direction the yellow car is moving / the red car changes shape

Assessment

A more formal assessment of the students' understanding of the topic can be undertaken using Assessment Sheets P1, P2 and P3. These can be completed in class, or as a homework task.

Students following Cambridge Assessment International Education Primary Science Curriculum Framework will write progression tests set and supplied by Cambridge at this level and feedback will be given regarding their achievement levels.

Assessment Sheet answers

Sheet P1
1. pull / push / twist [3]
2. wind [1]
3. The small boat with large sails. [1]
4. push / harder / bigger / faster / do not move [5]

Sheet P2
1. false / false [2]
1. a force
   b force [2]
3. large / moving [2]
4. water / turn / push / force [4]

Sheet P3
1. squash / stretch / squeeze [3]
2. true / false [2]
3. 5 N / 8 N [2]
4. squeeze / stretch / shape [3]

Student's Book answers

Pages 72–73
1. Push toys – trolley, tricycle
   Pull toys – duck, cart, helicopter, pull-along toy
2. Our arms.
3. They move.
4. The object moves (phone button depresses, trolley moves forward, ox moves plough).
5. Pulling the plough.
6. Check students' answers.

Pages 74–75
1. The car and the ball.
2. The spinning top.
3. The windmill can move without being touched (by blowing it/the wind).
4. They will not move.
5. The red car.
6. The green car.
7. The green car, as it has travelled furthest.

Pages 76–77
1. The sailing ship.
2. The boats stop moving.
3. If the wind was stronger or if the boat had bigger sails.
4. The force of the wind.
5. If the wind was stronger or the windmill had bigger sails.
6. Because it uses a natural force and saves human effort.
7. They rely on the wind – if there is no wind they don't work.
8. The force of the water.

Pages 78–79
1. It stretches.
2. It stretches more.
3. The spring could stretch too far and break.
4. Because it measures forces in units called newtons.
5. The stone.
6. The small metal horse.
7. The small metal horse.

Pages 80–81
1. The second picture.
   It knocked the goalkeeper over.
2. The second picture.
3. It could hurt someone.

Pages 82–83
1. 1 The goalie heads the ball, so it changes direction. 2 The man kicks the ball and it starts moving. 3 The goalie catches the ball, so it stops moving.
2. The goalie applies a force with his head.
3. start moving / stop moving
4. the axe is swinging downward / the car is travelling forward / the ball is travelling forward towards the racket / the branch is travelling forward towards the waterfall
5. it hits the tree / it is hit by another car / it is hit by the racket / it is pushed down by the waterfall
6. stopping / sideways and forward / backwards / downwards

Pages 84–85
1. The baker is kneading (stretching) dough to make bread.
2. squash / stretch
3. It has been hit by something. The metal has changed shape.
4. No, some materials are elastic.
5. elasticity
6. It has been hit by the hammer.
7. It is not easy because metal is a strong and hard material.
8. Forces can shape the metal to make car parts.

Pages 86–87
1. A rubbing force between two surfaces that slows things down.
2. There would be less friction, so she would move faster and perhaps even slip.
3. My hand pushes the book forwards. Friction from the desk surface pushes backwards.
4. It will fall. Gravity is the force acting on it now.

1.4 Plants need sunlight

PCM B1: Planning an investigation

Our question is:
How does the amount of sunlight affect the growth of plants?

Our prediction is:

What are we changing?

What are we measuring?

What are we keeping the same to make the test fair?

What are we going to do?

Stage 3 Collins Primary Science 2014

1.4 Plants need sunlight

PCM B2: **Shoebox maze**

> **You will need:**
> - shoebox with lid
> - extra cardboard
> - scissors
> - sticky tape
> - small potted plant (bean plant)

1. Cut a large hole at one end of the shoebox. Hold the box up to the light and be sure to tape up any other spaces where light shines through.

2. Cut two pieces of cardboard. Make them half the width of the shoebox and the same height as the shoebox.

3. Mark the box into thirds and tape one cardboard piece on the left side of the box at the one-third mark. Next, tape the other cardboard piece on the right side of the box at the two-thirds mark.

4. Place a small potted plant in the shoebox. Make sure that it is well watered.

5. Close the box, tape on its lid and place it in a sunny position for one week.

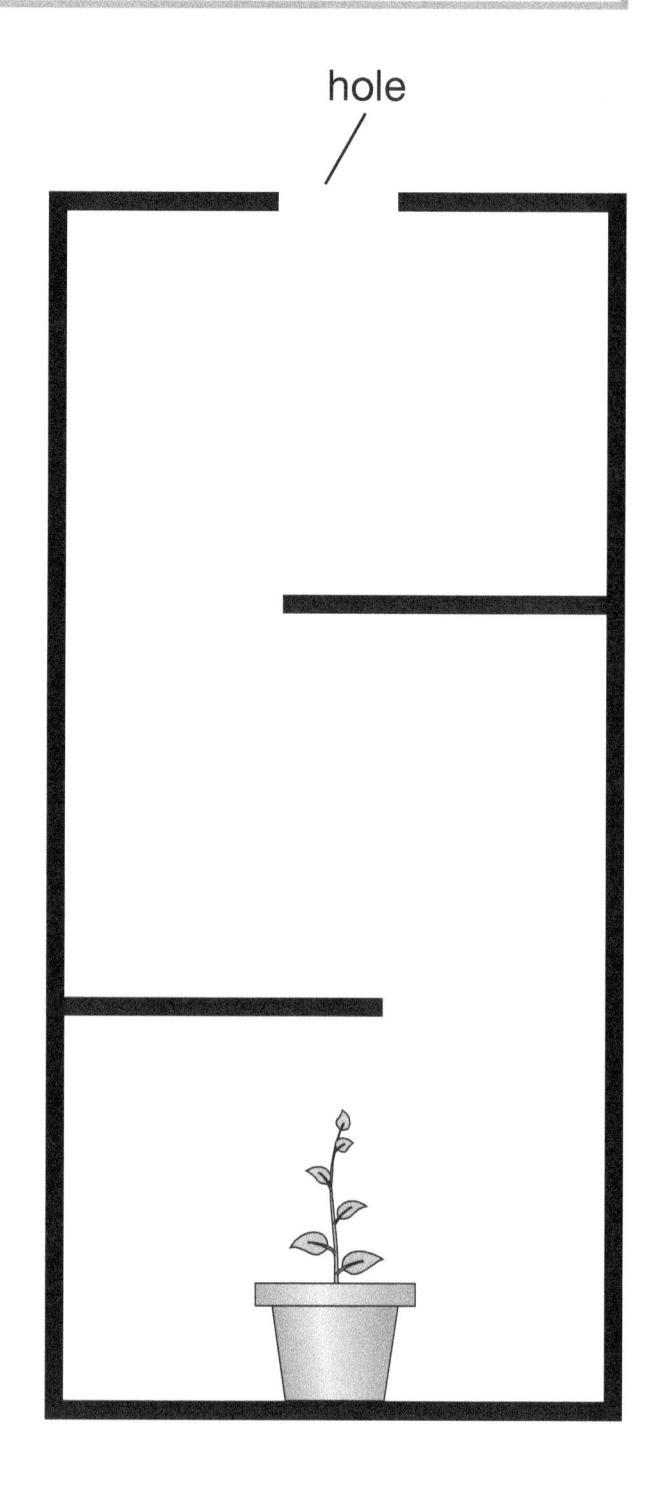

hole

92 Stage 3 Collins Primary Science 2014

1.5 Making food

PCM B3: **Plants in the environment**

1 Nawal and Noura are growing plants in different conditions.

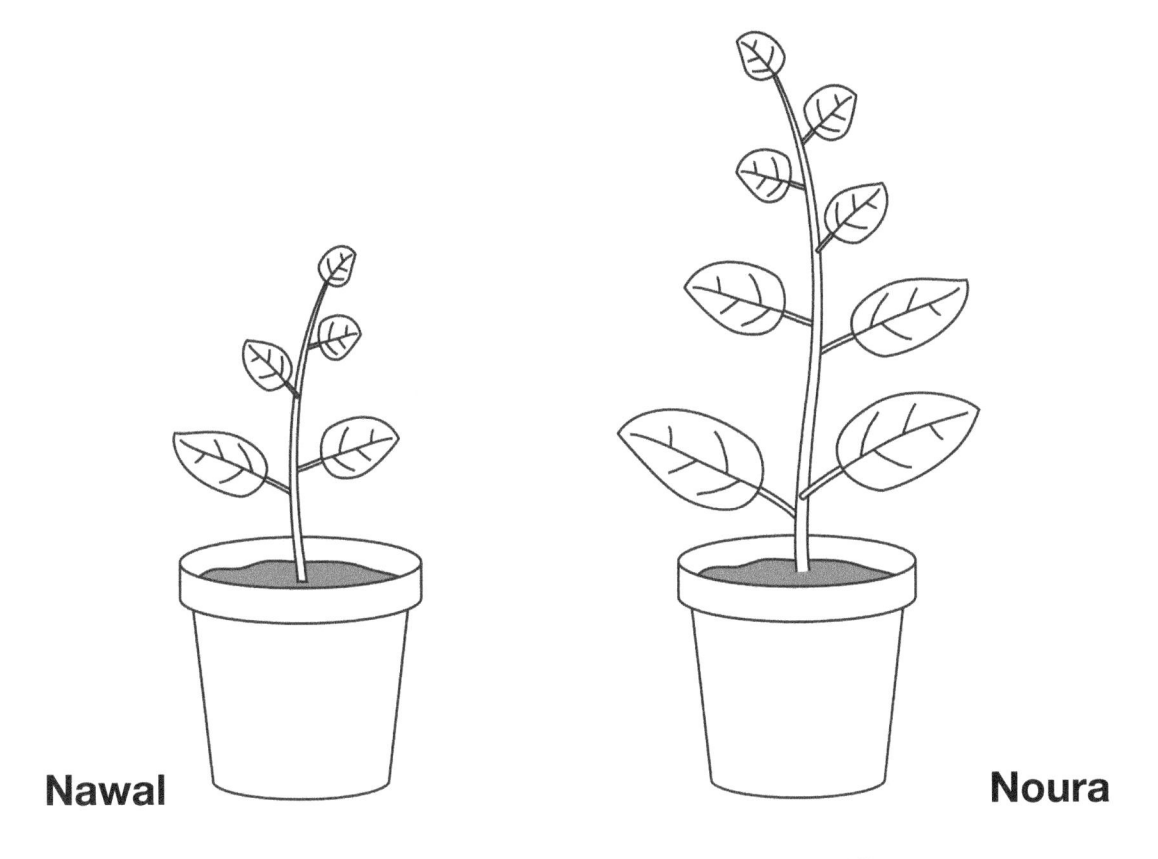

Nawal   **Noura**

- Which plant is growing on a sunny windowsill? _____

- How can you tell? _____

2 What order do plant parts grow in? Write the numbers from 2 to 5. The first step is done for you.
- flower ___
- shoot _1_
- root ___
- seed ___
- stem ___

3 Name one type of root we eat. _____

4 Find three things that roots do. Circle your answers.
- collect sunlight
- take in water
- to hold the plant in the soil
- take in minerals
- collect soil
- take in air

Stage 3 Collins Primary Science 2014   93

1.8 Plants in the desert

PCM B4: Matching plants to their habitats

cactus – thin spiny leaves so it does not lose moisture, fat stem to store water

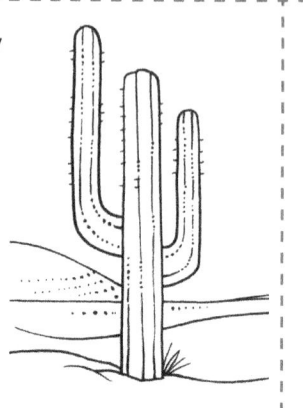

mangrove – leaves can get rid of salt water, long roots to anchor the plant, seeds float

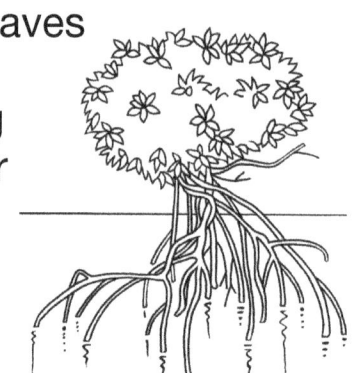

alpine – shallow roots, short stems, grows close to the ground, able to survive underneath the snow in winter

strangler fig – long roots grow downwards to the soil, long stems grow up towards the light

desert – hot and dry

coastal mangrove – soft soil, salty water

mountain – cold, not much soil, strong winds, snow in winter

rainforest – hot, wet, dark

Stage 3 Collins Primary Science 2014

PCM B5: Food groups

1 Cut along the dotted lines and shuffle the cards.

2 Match each food group to examples of that food group, and then to what the food group does.

Milk Meat Fish Eggs Nuts Cheese Peas and beans	**Proteins**	Help you to grow strong hair and nails
Bread Pasta Rice Potatoes	**Carbohydrates**	Give you energy
Butter Olive oil Ghee Cheese	**Fats**	Give you energy Protect internal organs Keeps the body warm in cooler temperatures
Cabbage, spinach, tomatoes, beans Apples, oranges, grapes, bananas	**Fruit and vegetables**	Full of vitamins and minerals Keep you healthy Prevent illness
Chocolates Sweets Fruit	**Sugars**	Give you energy

Stage 3 Collins Primary Science 2014

2.7 Your senses

PCM B6: Testing your senses

Our question is:

Our prediction is:

What are we changing?

What are we going to do?

What are we measuring?

What are we keeping the same to make the test fair?

PCM B7: Animal groups

1. Write each definition under the name of the correct animal group.
2. Then research the animal groups and write in any sub-groups you learn about.

Animals

Fish	Reptiles	Mammals
Amphibians	**Birds**	**Insects**

- Have a beak, two wings and two legs. They are covered in feathers.
- Live on land and in water.
- Have dry scales that cover their bodies.
- Have six legs.
- Mostly live on land, although some live in water. They feed on their mother's milk when they are young.
- Live in water. They have gills to breathe and fins to help them move.

2.10 Classifying living things (2)

Stage 3 Collins Primary Science 2014

3.1 Properties of materials

PCM C1: Sorting materials

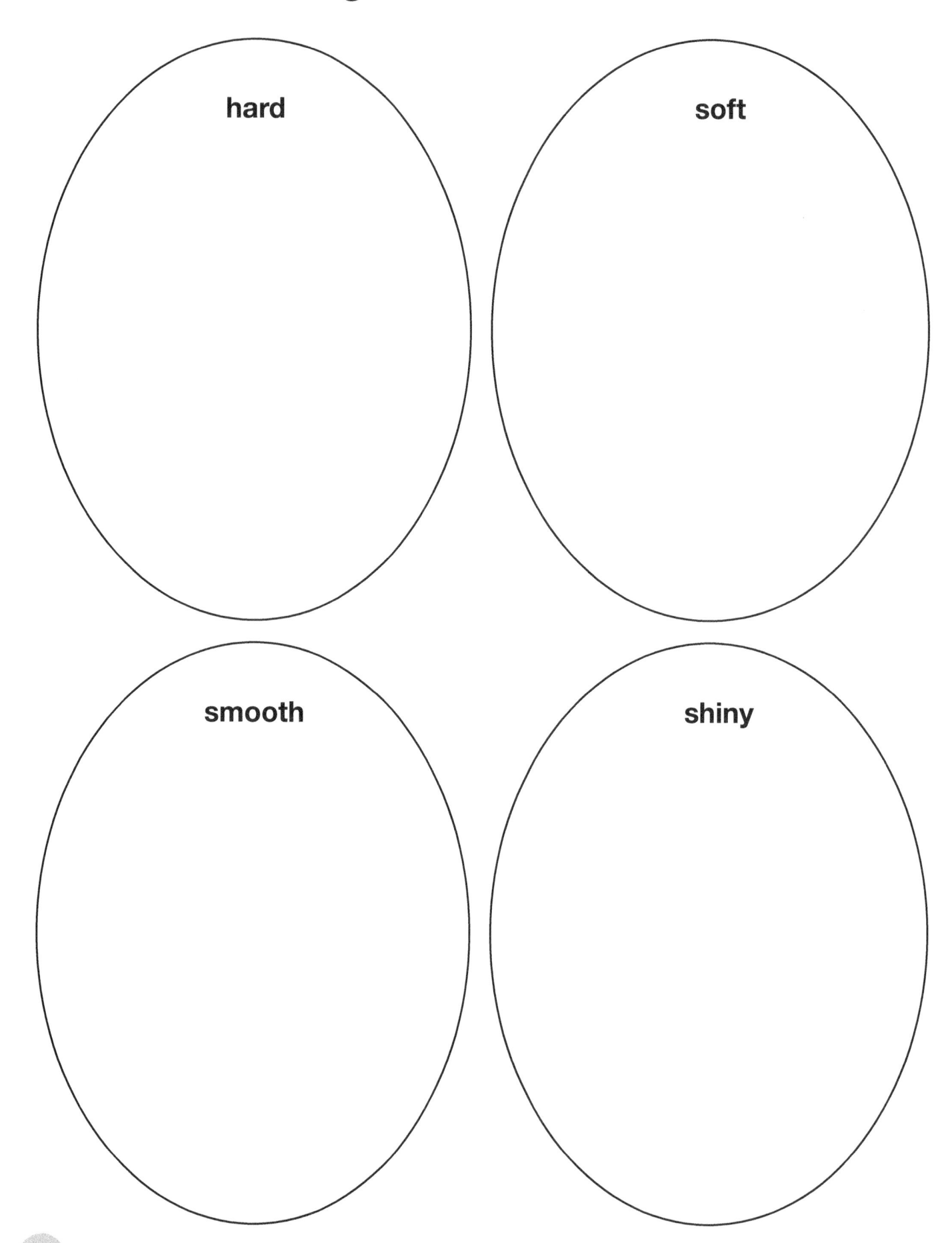

hard

soft

smooth

shiny

PCM C2: Strong or weak?

Strong	Weak

3.4 Flexibility

PCM C3: How flexible?

Set up the equipment as shown in the diagram.

Predict which material is the most flexible.

Then hang masses from each material to test your predictions.

Record the results in a table.

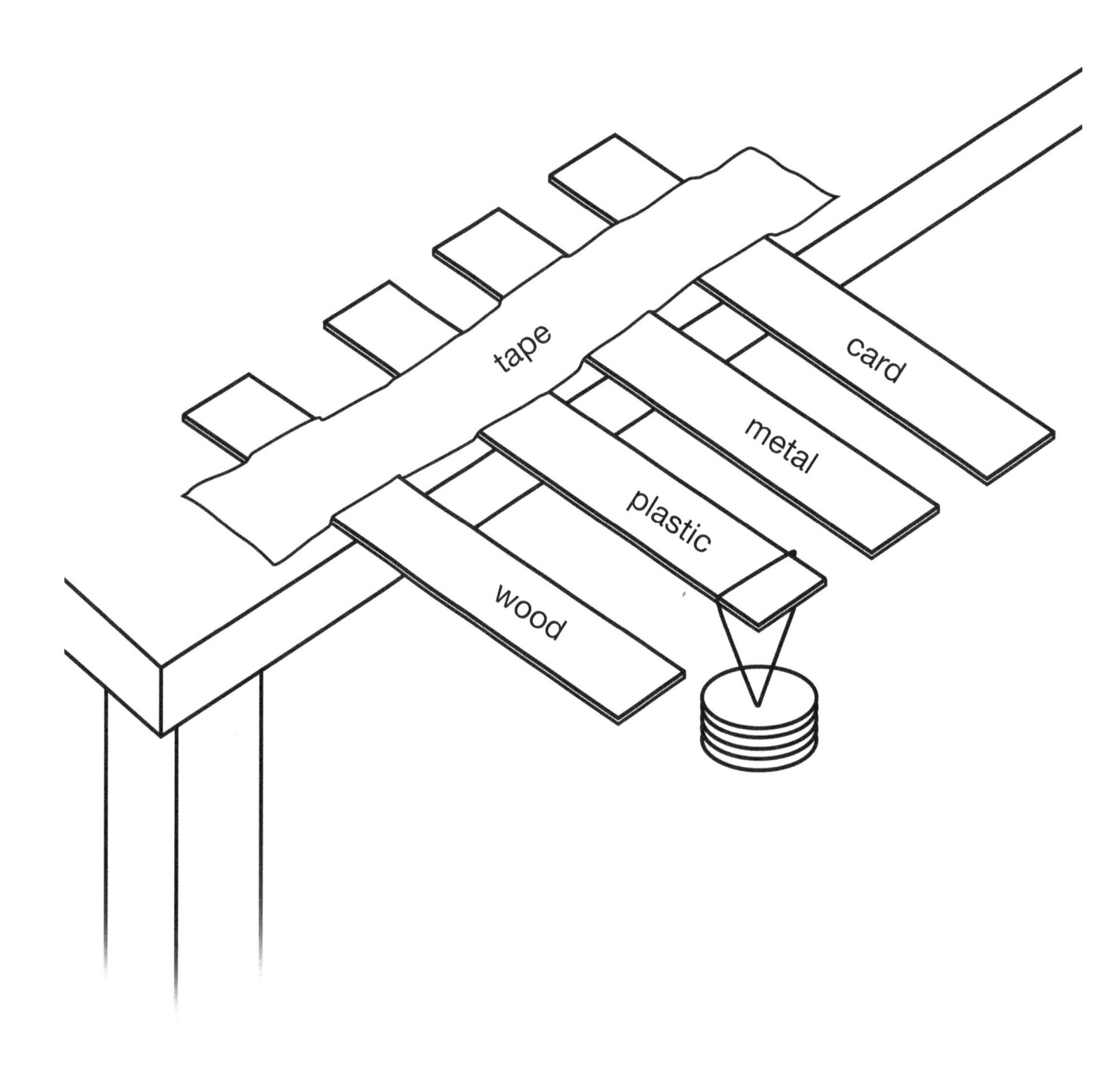

PCM C4: Does shape affect strength?

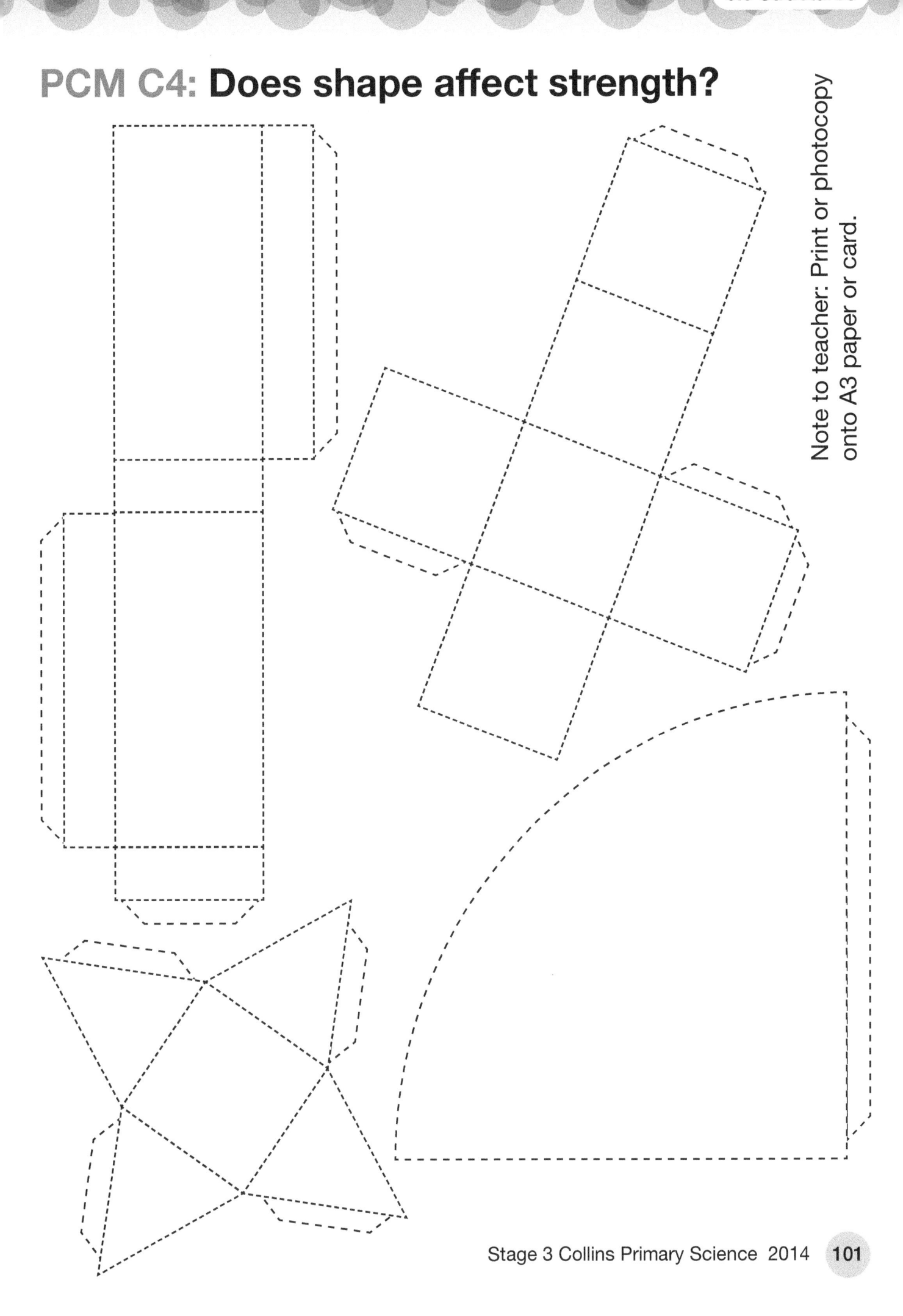

Note to teacher: Print or photocopy onto A3 paper or card.

Stage 3 Collins Primary Science 2014 101

3.5 Structures

3.6 Uses of materials

PCM C5: Building materials

Look at the cards showing different materials, their properties and their uses. Match each material to its uses and its properties.

Material	Use	Property
Concrete	Bridges	Hard and difficult to break
Metal	Windows	Hard, long-lasting and waterproof
Slate	Table	Soft and easy to mould into different shapes, becomes hard when fired in a kiln
Wood	Foundations for buildings	Hard, easy to make into different shapes and nail together
Glass	Roofing tiles	See-through and brittle
Limestone	Bricks	Easy to mix, becomes hard, strong and long-lasting when set
Clay	Building blocks	Hard, easy to carve with a chisel, long-lasting

3.7 Staying the same shape

PCM C6: **Elastic materials**

What you will need
- loops of a variety of elastic materials such as rubber bands, tights, elastic bandage, stretch fabric, rope, hair band, rubber gloves
- standard small masses
- long ruler
- eye protection

Safety
Wear eye protection throughout this experiment. Warn them of the dangers of rubber bands breaking and masses falling.

Demonstrate how to use the equipment to the class.

1 Fasten some paper to the wall.

2 Draw a line at the top (line 1).

3 Hold the loop of material to be tested so that the top of the loop lines up with line 1 on the paper.

4 Draw a line on the paper to show how far down the loop reaches (line 2).

5 Next hang some weights on the loop and again hold it so the top of the loop lines up with line 1.

6 Draw another line to show how far down the wall the loop reaches now (line 3).

7 Measure the distance between line 2 and line 3 to see how far the material has stretched.

3.8 Floating or sinking?

PCM C7: Will it float?

Make these paper boats as small or as large as you want.

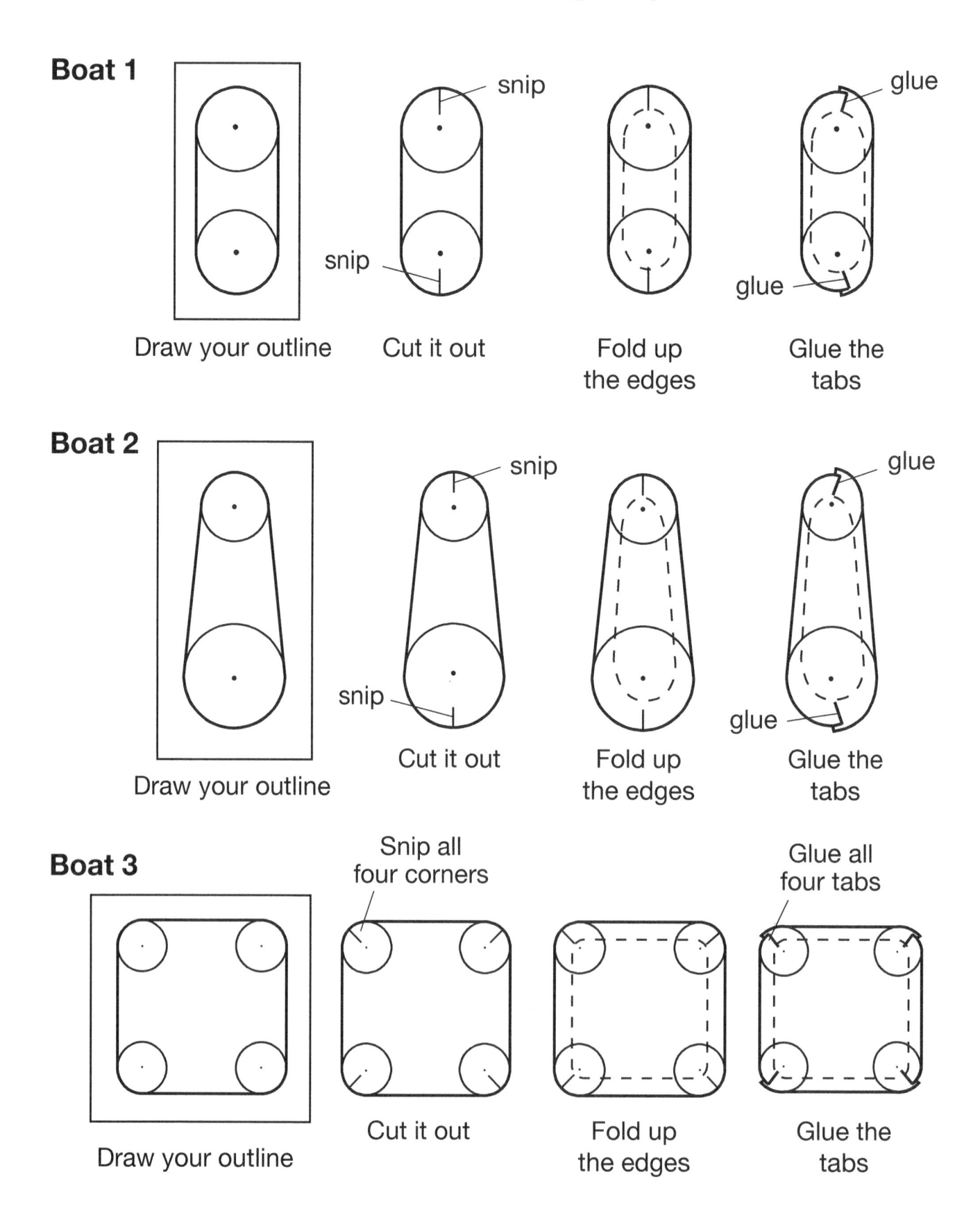

Boat 1

Draw your outline — Cut it out — Fold up the edges — Glue the tabs

snip, snip, glue, glue

Boat 2

Draw your outline — Cut it out — Fold up the edges — Glue the tabs

snip, snip, glue, glue

Boat 3

Draw your outline — Snip all four corners / Cut it out — Fold up the edges — Glue all four tabs / Glue the tabs

104 Stage 3 Collins Primary Science 2014

PCM C8: Testing magnets

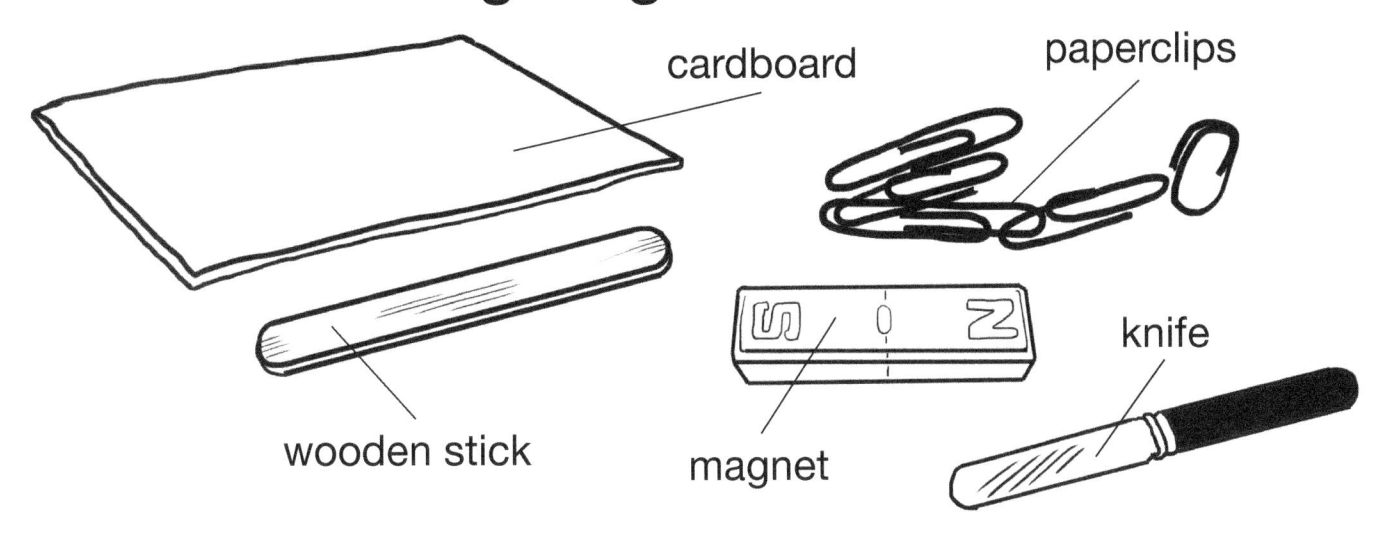

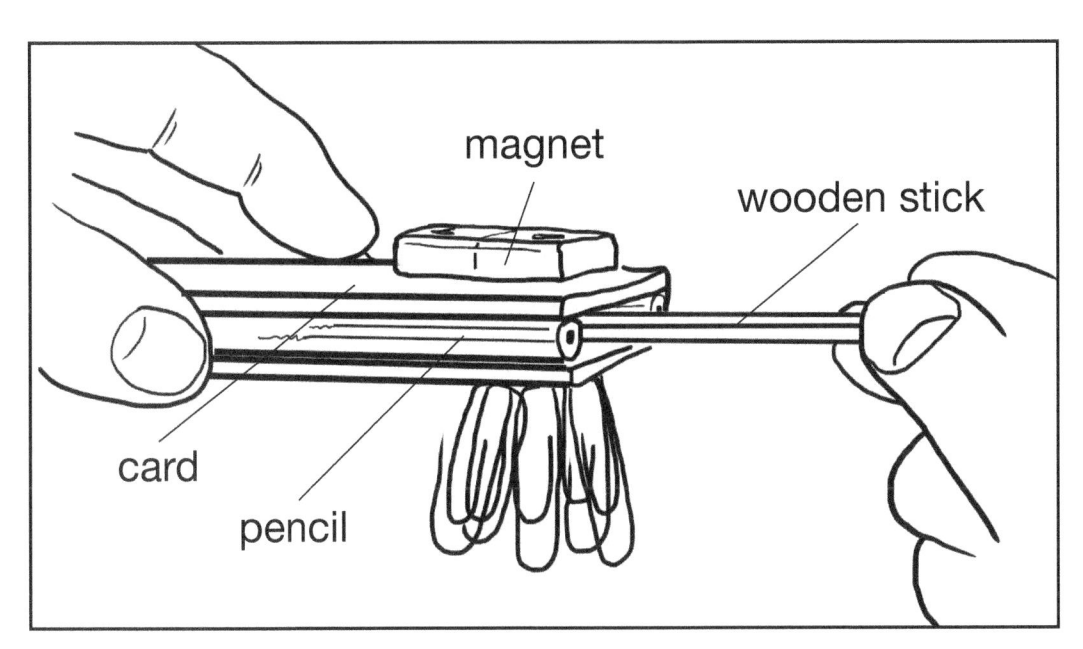

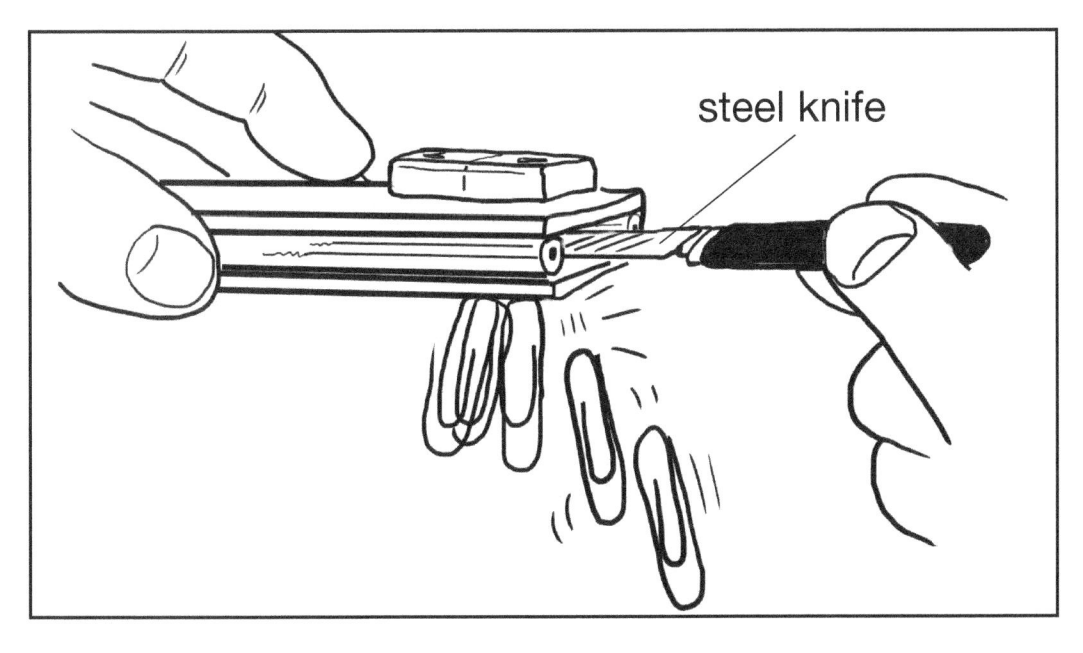

cardboard

paperclips

wooden stick

magnet

knife

magnet

wooden stick

card

pencil

steel knife

Stage 3 Collins Primary Science 2014

4.2 Making things move

PCM P1: Push, pull, twist

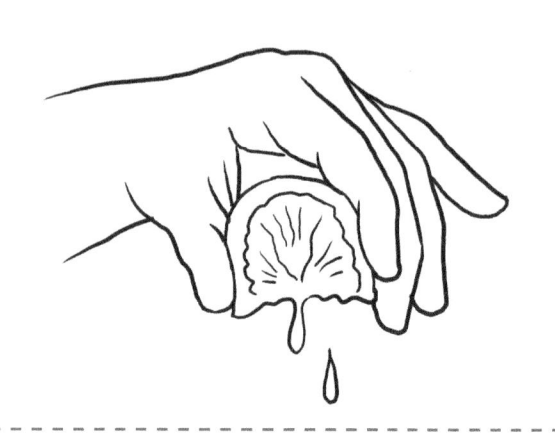

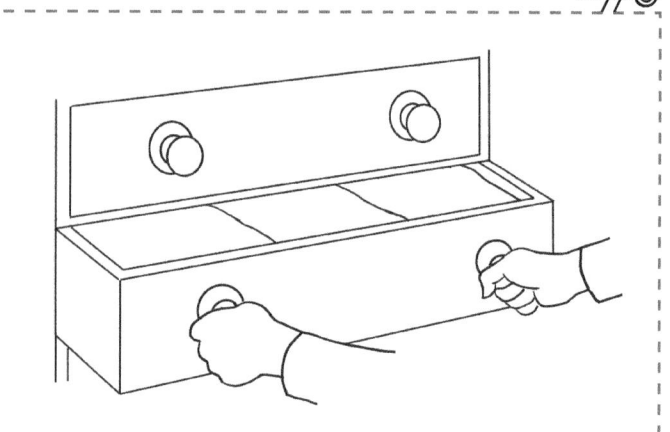

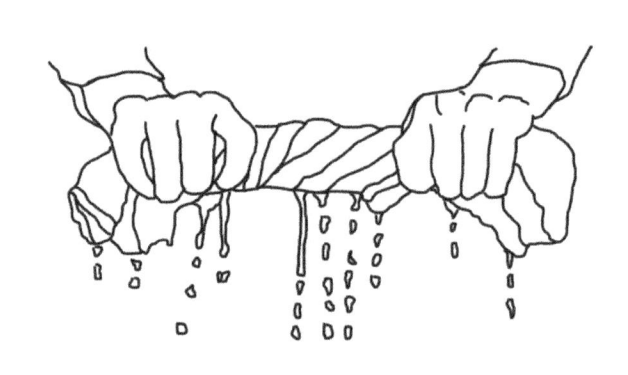

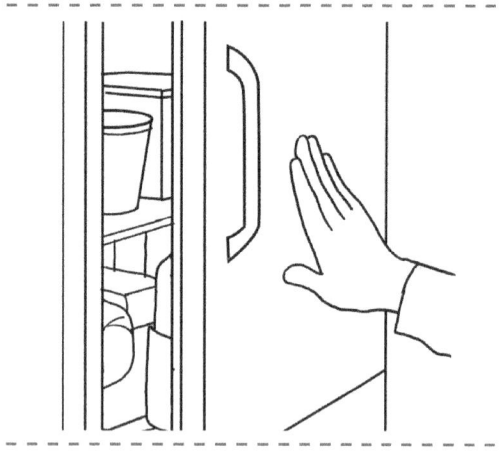

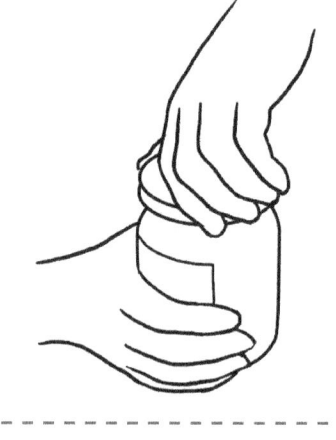

push	pull
push	pull
twist	twist

PCM P2: Springs and masses

1. Hang the spring from the rod.

2. Hook the mass hanger on the spring.

3. Measure the length of the spring with a strip of paper.

4. Label the strip of paper 'start'.

5. Add a mass to the mass hanger.

6. Measure the length of the spring again with a new strip of paper.

7. Label this strip 'one extra mass'.

8. Add another mass to the mass hanger.

9. Measure the length of the spring again with a new strip of paper.

10. Label this strip 'two extra masses'.

11. Add up to five masses to your mass hanger. Remember to measure the length with a new strip of paper each time.

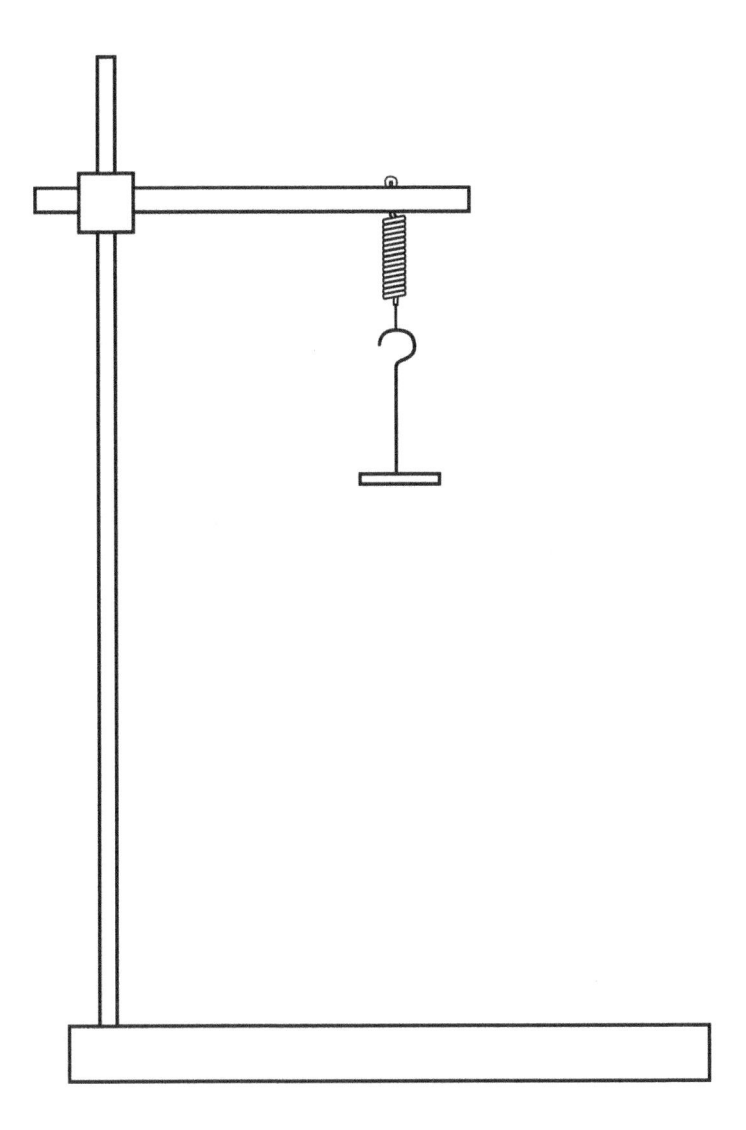

4.8 Friction

PCM P3: Bicycle brakes

Look at the pictures. They show how bicycle brakes work.

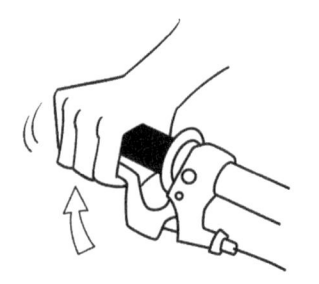

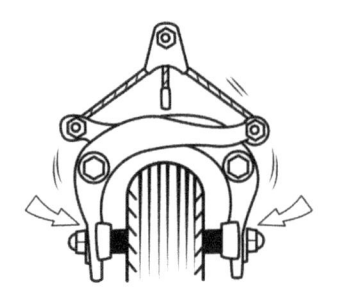

1 Add these mixed up labels to the pictures.

> The rubber block gets pressed against the wheel.
> You squeeze the brake lever.   The bike stops.
> Rubber block   Wheel   The metal hinge is pulled shut.

2 Now write a paragraph to explain how brakes work.

_____

_____

_____

_____

108   Stage 3 Collins Primary Science 2014

Biology: Assessment Sheet B1

1 Draw a line from each label to the part of the plant that does that job.

| sunlight is trapped and used by the plant to make food | | keeps the plant upright and transports water to the leaves |

| water is taken in from the soil | | these are often brightly coloured to attract insects |

[4 marks]

2 Read the statements. Circle either 'True' or 'False'.
Plants make their own food.
            TRUE / FALSE
Leaves have veins that carry water around the leaf.
            TRUE / FALSE
If a plant loses its leaves it cannot replace them.
            TRUE / FALSE   [3 marks]

3 Fill in the table to explain why water plants are often different to land plants.

Difference	Explanation
Water plants can have much weaker stems than land plants.	
Water plants can have much bigger leaves than land plants.	

[2 marks]

4 Describe the way in which changing the amount of light affects how a plant grows.

_____

_____ [1 mark]

[Total: _____ /10]

Topic 1 Plants

Biology: Assessment Sheet B2

1. Circle the correct words.

   Plant need **water / coffee** and **shade / sunlight** to grow. They also need **warmth / clothes**. Seeds won't grow if they are in a very **cold / dusty** place.
   The **thermometer / temperature** has to be warm enough for them to start growing. [5 marks]

2. Write down two reasons why plants are important for animals.

   _____

   _____ [2 marks]

3. Read the statements. Circle either 'True' or 'False'.

   All flowers have the same number of petals.
   TRUE / FALSE

   Plants make their own food.
   TRUE / FALSE

   Roots take in soil and stones and transport them to the leaves.
   TRUE / FALSE [3 marks]

   [Total: _____ /10]

Topic 1 Plants

Biology: Assessment Sheet B3

1 Complete the sentences using the words in the box.

   | tap roots   fibrous roots   stores   water |

   Some roots grow deep into the soil. These are called

   _____. Other roots spread out widely to

   capture as much _____ as possible.

   These roots are called _____. The roots

   of some plants become very fat, because the plant

   _____ food in them. [4 marks]

2 Read the statements. Circle either 'True' or 'False'.

   Trees are plants.   TRUE / FALSE

   The stem of a tree is called a trunk.   TRUE / FALSE

   Flowers are brightly coloured to make us pick them.
                                                  TRUE / FALSE   [3 marks]

3 Write down two reasons why a cactus is suited to growing in the desert.

   _____

   _____ [2 marks]

4 Name an insect that carries pollen from one flower to another.

   _____ [1 mark]

   [Total: _____/10]

Stage 3 Collins Primary Science 2014   111

Topic 2 Humans and animals

Biology: Assessment Sheet B4

1 Tick (✓) the living things.

[2 marks]

2 Draw a line from each animal in Group A to a fact about it in Group B.

Group A
bird
amphibian
mammal
insect

Group B
have fur
can fly
live near water
have six legs   [4 marks]

3 Which sense organ is being used in each of these activities?

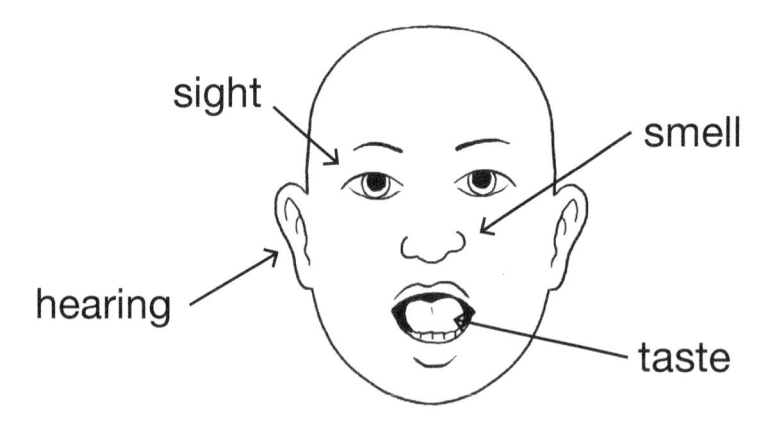

The painting looks beautiful. _____

The flowers smell nice. _____

I can hear the baby crying. _____

This drink is sweet. _____   [4 marks]

[Total: _____ /10]

Topic 2 Humans and animals

Biology: Assessment Sheet B5

1 Read the statements. Circle either 'True' or 'False'.

Fish have scales.	TRUE / FALSE
A horse is an insect.	TRUE / FALSE
Humans are mammals.	TRUE / FALSE

[3 marks]

2 Tick (✓) the mammals.

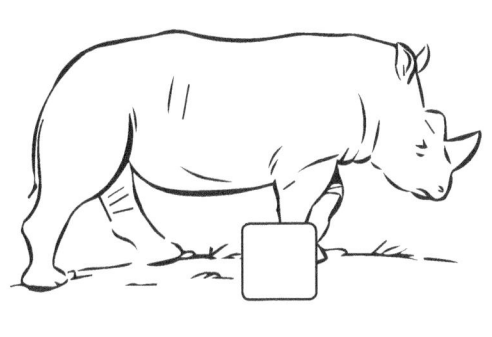

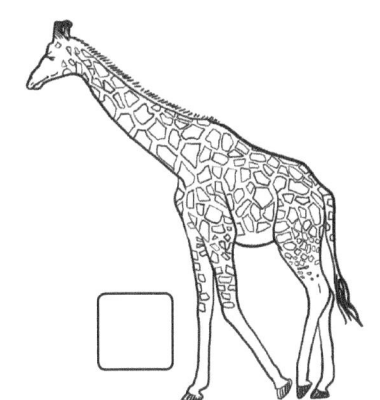

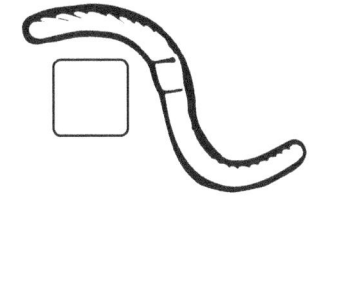

[3 marks]

3 Circle the correct words.

Your body uses **energy / electricity** to read, stay alive, grow and move. This comes from **food / cars** . Different kinds of foods provide different things for your body. Milk and cheese help you to grow and develop strong bones. They are in the food group called **protein / photosynthesis** . You should eat lots of **sweets / vegetables** every day to stay healthy.

[4 marks]

[Total: _____/10]

Stage 3 Collins Primary Science 2014   113

Topic 2 Humans and animals

Biology: **Assessment Sheet B6**

1 Write about three different ways your senses can help you.

_____

_____

_____ [3 marks]

2 Draw or write the name of a food for each food group listed in the table.

Protein	
Fats	
Carbohydrates	
Sugars	
Fruit and vegetables	

[5 marks]

3 Circle the correct words.

Exercise builds strong **teeth / muscles** and bones, and

is good for your **heart / hair** . [2 marks]

[Total: _____ /10]

114   Stage 3 Collins Primary Science 2014

Chemistry: Assessment Sheet C1

1 Circle the magnetic materials.

iron   plastic   wood   steel   [2 marks]

2 Draw a line from each object in Group A to a description in Group B.

Group A
wooden spoon
drinks can
mirror
T-shirt

Group B
round and smooth
hard and rough
soft and flexible
shiny and flat   [4 marks]

3 Circle the correct words.

A good material to build a bridge with is **metal / plastic** because it can take a very heavy **load / stretch** and will last for many years.

A good material to make a table with is **wood / paper** because it is **strong / flexible** but easy to shape with tools. [4 marks]

[Total: _____/10]

Topic 3 Material properties

Chemistry: Assessment Sheet C2

1. Circle two properties that help objects to float.

   colour   texture   shape

   shiny   hollow   weight   [2 marks]

2. Tick (✓) the properties that are important for an aquarium.

   see-through ☐

   flexible ☐

   strong ☐

   waterproof ☐

   soft ☐   [3 marks]

3. Name a way to test how hard a material is. Choose the correct word from the box.

   The _____ test.

soft   sharp   red   rub

   [1 mark]

4. Read the statements. Circle either 'True' or 'False'.

   Inflatable life jackets are made from flexible materials.
        TRUE / FALSE

   Metal is a good material to use for an inflatable life jacket.
        TRUE / FALSE

   Materials that stretch and then go back to their original shape are called elastic materials.   TRUE / FALSE

   If a material is waterproof it will let water through.
        TRUE / FALSE   [4 marks]

   [Total: _____ /10]

Topic 3 Material properties

Chemistry: **Assessment Sheet C3**

1 Draw a line from the beginning of each sentence to the end.

A hard material... ...do not break easily.

You can use the dent test... ...can scratch a soft one.

...to test the hardness of a material.

Strong materials...

[3 marks]

2 Look at the shapes and answer the questions.

a What is the name of shape A? _____

b Which shape is unstable? _____

c Draw a stable structure.

A

B

[3 marks]

4 Tick the sentence if it is true. Cross the sentence if it is false.

The shape of a building can make it more stable. ☐

Wood and metal are used in buildings. ☐

[2 marks]

5 Name two properties that wood and metal share.

_____

_____ [2 marks]

[Total: ____/10]

Topic 4 Forces and motion

Physics: Assessment Sheet P1

1. Label the drawings using the words in the box.

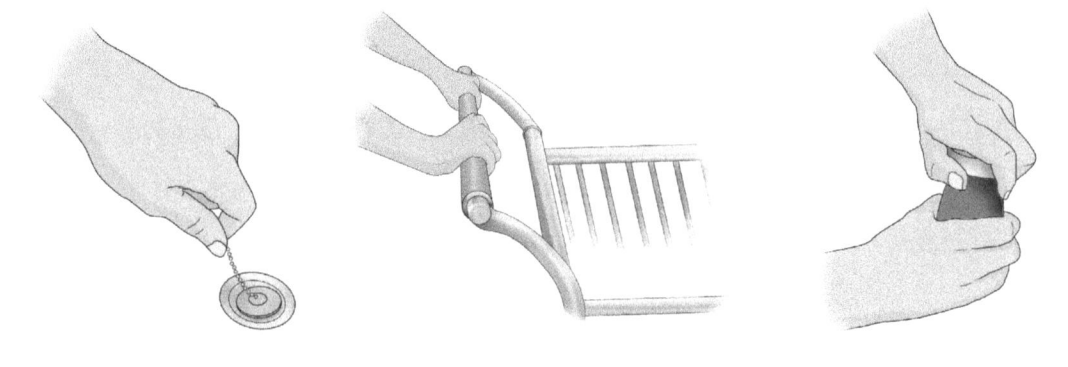

_____   _____   _____

| pull   twist   push |

[3 marks]

2. Name the force that pushes a boat's sails. _____ [1 mark]

3. Tick (✓) the boat that would move faster on a windy day.

   A big ship with small sails. ☐

   A small boat with large sails. ☐   [1 mark]

4. Look at the picture. Circle the correct words.

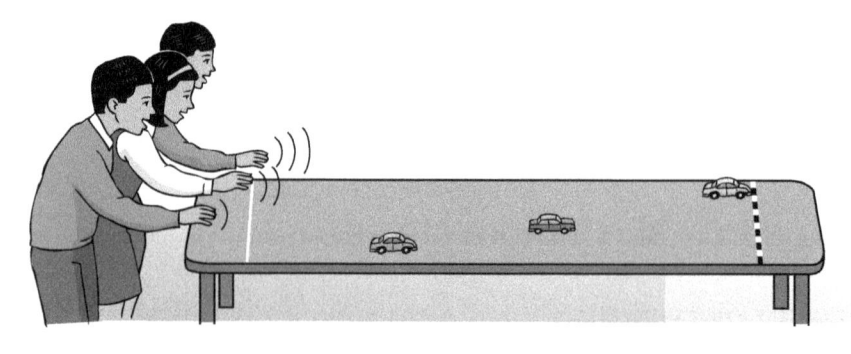

The children are racing toy cars. They give them a **push / pull** with their hands to make them move. If they push **heavier / harder** it gives a **bigger / fatter** force. This makes their cars move **faster / slower**. If they do not push at all their cars **do not move / move slower**.

[5 marks]

[Total: _____/10]

118   Stage 3 Collins Primary Science 2014

Topic 4 Forces and motion

Physics: Assessment Sheet P2

1 Look at the pictures. Circle either 'True' or 'False'.

The tennis ball is larger than the balloon.   TRUE / FALSE
The balloon is heavier than the tennis ball. TRUE / FALSE   [2 marks]

2 a What does this object measure?

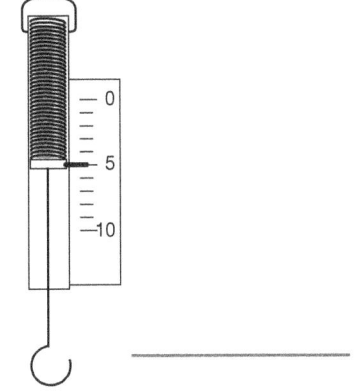

b Complete this sentence. Choose the correct word from the box.

Newtons are a measurement of _____ .

| temperature   mass   force |

[2 marks]

3 Circle the correct words.

Fast-moving objects need a **large / small** force to make them stop.

A force can stop something from **growing / moving** .   [2 marks]

4 Write about how a waterwheel works. Use the words in the box.

| push   force   water   turn |

_____ is used to _____ a water wheel.

Water can _____ with a very strong _____ .   [4 marks]

[Total: _____/10]

Stage 3 Collins Primary Science 2014   119

Topic 4 Forces and motion

Physics: Assessment Sheet P3

1 Label the pictures using force words from the box.

| push   pull   squash   squeeze   stretch |

[3 marks]

2 Read the statements. Circle either 'True' or 'False'.

Friction is a rubbing force that slows things down.
                                    TRUE /FALSE

Gravity is the force that pushes objects away from the Earth.
                                    TRUE / FALSE   [2 marks]

3 Look at the pictures. Read the scale on each newton meter.

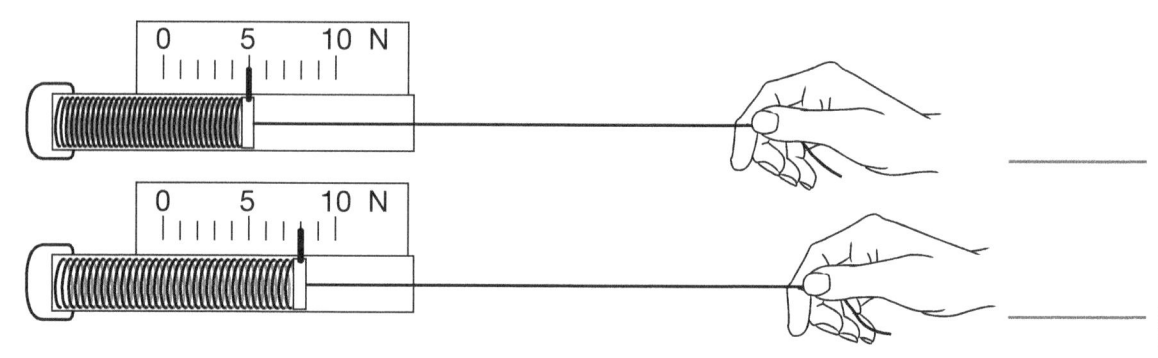

[2 marks]

4 Complete the sentences using the words in the box.

| shape   squeeze   stretch |

Forces can change the shape of some things. You

can _____ a ball in your hand, and it changes shape.

You can _____ an elastic band, and it changes shape.

You can fold a sheet of paper, and it changes _____ .   [3 marks]

[Total: _____/10]

120   Stage 3 Collins Primary Science 2014